Best Ever
PAPER
AIRPLANES

Norman Schmidt

Sterling Publishing Co., Inc. New York

A Sterling/Tamos Book

A Sterling/Tamos Book
© 1994 by Norman Schmidt

Published in Paperback in 2007 by Sterling Publishing Co., Inc.
387 Park Avenue South, New York, N.Y. 10016

TAMOS Books Inc.
300 Wales Avenue, Winnipeg, MB, Canada R2M 2S9

10 9 8 7 6 5 4

Distributed in Canada by Sterling Publishing
c/o Canadian Manda Group, 165 Dufferin Street
Toronto, Ontario, Canada M6K 3H6
Distributed in the United Kingdom by GMC Distribution Services
Castle Place, 166 High Street, Lewes, East Sussex, England BN7 1XU
Distributed in Australia by Capricorn Link (Australia) Pty. Ltd.
P.O. Box 704, Windsor, NSW 2756, Australia

Design   Norman Schmidt
Photography   Jerry Grajewski & Walter Kaiser,
                KKS Commercial Photography
Printed in China 10 / 10

CANADIAN CATALOGING IN PUBLICATION DATA

Schmidt, Norman Jacob, 1947-
  Best ever paper airplanes

  Includes index.
  ISBN 1-895569-20-6

1. Paper Airplanes.   I. Title.
TL778.S35 1994   745.592   C93-098175-8

LIBRARY OF CONGRESS
CATALOGING IN PUBLICATION DATA

Schmidt, Norman.
  Best ever paper airplanes / Norman Schmidt.
      p.   cm.
  "A Sterling/Tamos book."
  ISBN 1-895569-20-6
  1.Paper airplanes – juvenile literature
  [1. Paper airplanes. 2. Flight.]   I. Title
TL778.S36   1994   93-39122
745.592 – dc20   CIP
                                         AC

Sterling ISBN-13: 978-1-895569-83-4
        ISBN-10: 1-895569-83-4

For information about customs editions, special sales, or premium
and corporate purchases, please contact Sterling Special Sales
Department at 800-805-5489 or specialsales@sterlingpub.com.

Contents

The advice and directions given in this book
have been carefully checked, prior to
printing, by the Author as well as the
Publisher. Nevertheless, no guarantee can
be given as to project outcome due to
possible differences in material and the
Author and Publisher will not
be responsible for
the results.

The Experience of Flight

We humans are unable to fly, except in our dreams. We can walk and run when our feet are on the ground and some of us can even move about weightlessly in water, but we are not equipped to be buoyed up in air. No amount of flapping of arms and kicking of legs will get us airborne.

Yet this has not dampened our enthusiasm for flight. We look longingly at the soaring birds and wonder how to imitate the magical experience. For us it is possible only through the application of technology. We must create a machine to do what birds do naturally.

Being airborne, whether it is a bird or an airplane, presents the beauty of an object in harmony with nature. We can recreate this experience when we build a tiny paper airplane, launch it, and watch it fly. Eighteen models, each named for a bird, are included in this book. Their plans are arranged in order of complexity – from simple to more involved. Each has been tested for flight.

All the airplanes in this book can be built using ordinary 20 or 24 lb bond copier paper measuring 8-1/2 in by 11 in (21.6cm by 27.9cm). It is available in a variety of colors but black paper may have to be purchased from an art store. Bond paper is lightweight, easy to cut and fold, and easy to fasten together; however, paper airplanes can be bent out of shape with use and therefore require constant adjustments in order to fly well.

Decorating Patterns for decorating the airplane are included in this book. They can be copied or modified, or you can create your own designs.

A very fine black felt-tipped permanent marker to draw the pattern works well (water-based markers wrinkle the paper). Narrow colored markers can be used to fill in. The letters and numbers on the planes can be made with an ordinary stencil.

It is easier to decorate the plane before it is completely assembled. However, you may wish to construct an undecorated trial plane to make sure it flies well. Once you have mastered the design, decorate as you construct it.

Flying Safely Some of the airplanes have sharp points so never fly them toward another person. If you fly the airplanes outdoors they may go farther than you expect. Be sure they do not go into the street where you will have to retrieve them.

How Airplanes Fly

In free flight all airplanes are acted upon by four forces working in pairs – lift/gravity and thrust/drag. In order to make successful airplanes it is important to understand how these forces work. Since air holds the planes up, that is our first concern.

Like every object in the world, air is made up of small, solid, evenly spaced particles called molecules. Air molecules are quite far apart compared to those that make up metal, wood, or paper and they are easily separated when we move through them. The particles are piled up in a thick layer from the ground, and this is called the atmosphere. It forms part of the space around us and the sky above us. This layer of air (atmosphere) exerts pressure on everything in the world and it is this pressure that makes flight possible.

THRUST

Vertical
Tail

Horizontal
Tail

Fuselage

LIFT

Wings

DRAG

GRAVITY

Lift An airplane or a bird becomes buoyant in air when a layer of reduced air pressure is created above the wings. This is accomplished when a wing having a curved upper surface moves forward and slices the air into two layers — one above and one beneath the wing. The air layers are made up of the same number of molecules, but those that travel over the curved top of the wing have farther to go. They must speed up and spread farther apart which causes them to exert less downward pressure. The molecules of air beneath the wing remain more closely spaced and thus buoy up the airplane. If the leading edge of the wing is raised slightly (the angle of attack), the difference in pressure above and below the wing is increased, adding more buoyancy.

Gravity This force pulls everything in the world to the ground. The lift created by the wings of an airplane in flight is opposed by the force of gravity. So the airplane's center of gravity (the point at which an object balances) must coincide with the lift created by the wings. If the plane's center of gravity is too far back the nose will pitch up; if too far forward the nose will pitch down.

Drag When air moves we can see it bending grass and trees. Even on a calm day we feel air pressing against us when we run or ride our bikes. Drag is the resistance air gives when we move through it. Because of drag it is hard work to pedal your bike very fast. Drag is also responsible for slowing down a paper airplane.

Thrust This is the forward momentum of an airplane. After you launch a paper airplane the force of lift prevents gravity from pulling the plane straight down. In flight the nose should point down only slightly. Then gravity adds to thrust. If the nose is pointed down too much the plane will crash into the ground. In free flight gravity will pull the plane along an invisible mass of air in downward gliding movement, just as gravity pulls a sled down a hill.

6

LIFT

Layer of reduced air pressure

Cross-section of wing

Angle of attack

Layer of air buoying the wing up

It is important to get the center of gravity in the correct spot. The planes in this book are designed with the correct center of gravity location, but if more ballast is needed, it may be added to the nose (use a small dab of plasticine, some clear tape, or a small pin). For best construction results use the 20 or 24 lb bond copier paper recommended, measure accurately, make crisp folds, and use glue sparingly.

While an airplane is in flight the four forces (lift/gravity and thrust/drag) must be in balance. Then the airplane is in *trim* for straight and level flight. Paper airplanes need frequent small adjustments to the control surfaces in order to fly well. You may need to make different trim adjustments for indoor flight than for outdoor flight in lively air.

Here are some common problems and solutions:

If the airplane zooms nose down to the ground, bend the elevators up slightly to raise the nose in flight.

This may cause the nose of the plane to pitch up sharply. As a result the air no longer flows smoothly over the wing surfaces but separates into eddies and the wings stall. Bend the elevators up less to adjust this problem.

If the elevators are not bent at all and the nose rises causing a stall, don't bend the elevators down (a plane should never fly this way). Rather add a bit of ballast to the nose.

If the plane veers to left or right, bend the aileron up slightly on the wing that rises and down slightly on the wing that falls. Also bend the rudder on the vertical tail slightly, opposite to the direction of the turn.

Always make small corrections. A small adjustment has a big effect.

Trimming for Flight

RUDDER ON VERTICAL TAIL
- trim for yaw and turn

ELEVATORS ON HORIZONTAL TAIL
- trim for nose up or down

AILERONS ON WING TIPS
- trim for bank and turn

THE CONTROL SURFACES

7

Basic Construction

The paper airplanes in this book are super flyers when carefully made. All paper airplanes need constant and careful trimming, but it is easier to trim a neatly constructed plane. Since a paper airplane's lift and thrust are limited, every effort must be made to keep drag at a minimum. Every surface not parallel to the direction of travel (wings, nose, and canopy) adds drag, so the neater and more accurate your construction, the better the plane will fly. Clean and accurate cuts and crisp folds are a top priority.

Measuring and Cutting Use a sharp pencil to mark the measurements and draw firm, accurate lines. Cut out the pieces with a sharp pair of scissors or a craft knife and a steel-edged ruler. A knife makes a cleaner cut.

Folding Always lay paper on a level surface for folding. Folding is easier along a score line (an indented line on the paper made with a hard pencil drawn along a ruler). There are four kinds of folds used in making the airplanes. They are mountain folds, valley folds, sink folds, and reverse folds. They are described on the opposite page.

Gluing A glue stick works well for paper airplanes. Cover the entire contacting surfaces that are to be joined. If there are multiple layers, apply glue to each of the sheets.

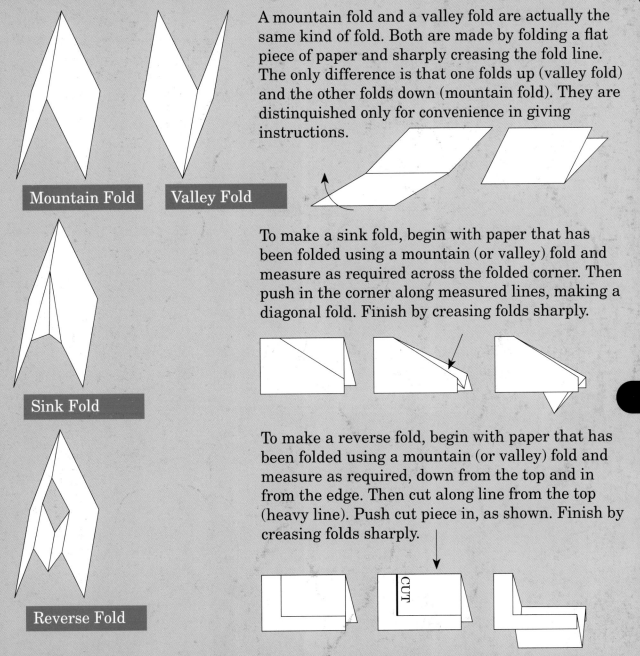

A mountain fold and a valley fold are actually the same kind of fold. Both are made by folding a flat piece of paper and sharply creasing the fold line. The only difference is that one folds up (valley fold) and the other folds down (mountain fold). They are distinquished only for convenience in giving instructions.

To make a sink fold, begin with paper that has been folded using a mountain (or valley) fold and measure as required across the folded corner. Then push in the corner along measured lines, making a diagonal fold. Finish by creasing folds sharply.

To make a reverse fold, begin with paper that has been folded using a mountain (or valley) fold and measure as required, down from the top and in from the edge. Then cut along line from the top (heavy line). Push cut piece in, as shown. Finish by creasing folds sharply.

CUT

Mountain Fold

Valley Fold

Sink Fold

Reverse Fold

Construction, Trim, and Launching

STRAIGHT PLANE

Air is deflected ONE way, rotating the plane about the center of gravity.

center of gravity

TWISTED PLANE

Air is deflected TWO ways. In order to rotate the plane about the center of gravity MORE trim is required.

center of gravity

dihedral angle

airplane lying on table

airplane in flight

Since folded paper twists easily, paper airplanes are not as straight as those of rigid construction. Shown above are two skinny airplane fuselages with deflected control surfaces (top view or side view). These demonstrate what a trim adjustment does in a straight airplane and in a twisted one. A twisted plane requires more trim, has more drag, and doesn't fly as well.

Instructions to make some of the planes in this book include a dihedral angle (the slant of the wings upward away from the fuselage). This keeps the plane from rolling. In some paper airplanes the dihedral angle is difficult to maintain in flight because fuselages flop open. Compensation for this must be made.

Before making any trim adjustments to a paper airplane be sure you are releasing it correctly for flight. Always begin with a gentle straight-ahead release, keeping the wings level. Suggested holding techniques are given in the directions. As your technique improves you can throw harder. All planes do not fly at the same speed.

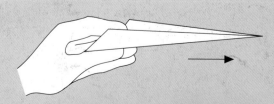

Glossary of Terms

Angle of attack The downward slant, from front to back, of a wing.

Angle of bank The raising of the outside wing and lowering of the inside wing during a turn.

Attitude The direction an airplane is pointing in relation to the horizon (banking, yawing, or pitching).

Control surfaces Small surfaces that can be bent to alter the airflow and change an airplane's attitude — ailerons for bank, elevators for pitch, and rudders for yaw.

Dihedral angle Upward slanting of wings away from the fuselage. (Downward slanting is called anhedral.)

Drag The resistance of air on moving objects, slowing them down.

Fuselage The body of an airplane.

Leading edges The front edges of wings, tails, or other parts.

Lift The force of air pressure beneath the wings buoying up an airplane.

Maneuver Skilfully making an airplane fly in a desired direction — turn, climb, dive, stall, spin, or loop.

Pitch Nose up or nose down attitude.

Roll Rotation along the length of an airplane.

Trailing edges The back edges of wings, tails, or other parts.

Trim Making small adjustments to the control surfaces to affect the attitude of an airplane.

Trim drag The drag (resistance) produced from bending control surfaces into the airflow.

Wing loading The amount of weight a given area of wing is required to lift.

Yaw Nose left or nose right attitude.

EGRET

#1

BACKGROUND INFORMATION

This airplane is called the "Egret" because of its slender shape and long nose. It is a delta (triangle) wing design. The plane looks like a flying triangle. Delta wings are used in slow-flying planes such as hang-gliders and high speed planes such as the Concord, which carries passengers faster than the speed of sound. Delta wings will probably be used in future planes that will carry passengers into space and back.

MAKING THE AIRPLANE

The Egret is constructed similarily to the common paper airplane that everyone makes. But because of this model's carefully measured shape, it can attain a very smooth and flat glide. Make sure that its shape is properly adjusted, with vertical tails straight up and down. Hold it between thumb and forefinger, launching it gently straight ahead.

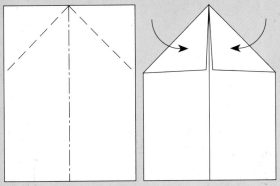

STEP 1 Lay paper flat in a vertical direction. Fold paper in half vertically using the mountain fold. Unfold. Then valley fold the upper corners to the center crease.

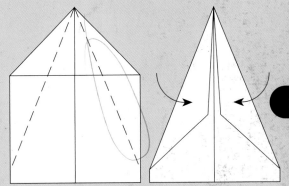

STEP 2 Valley fold the upper diagonals along broken lines to meet center crease.

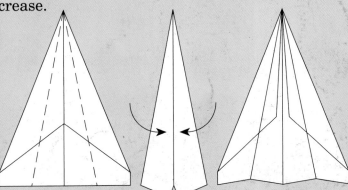

STEP 3 Valley fold outer edges along broken lines to meet the center crease. Unfold, as shown.

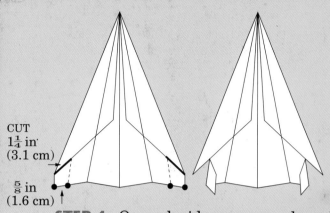

CUT
$1\frac{1}{4}$ in
(3.1 cm)

$\frac{5}{8}$ in
(1.6 cm)

STEP 4 On each side, measure along diagonal edge of paper, as shown by heavy line, and cut. Measure along bottom edge, in from each wing tip, and from this point, draw a line to the end of the cut. Valley fold along this line to make vertical tails.

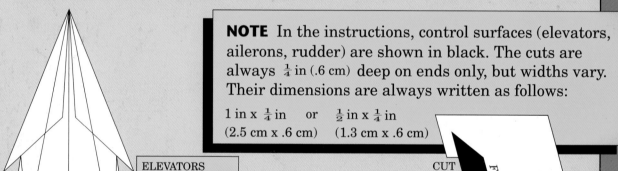

NOTE In the instructions, control surfaces (elevators, ailerons, rudder) are shown in black. The cuts are always $\frac{1}{4}$ in (.6 cm) deep on ends only, but widths vary. Their dimensions are always written as follows:

1 in x $\frac{1}{4}$ in   or $\frac{1}{2}$ in x $\frac{1}{4}$ in
(2.5 cm x .6 cm)   (1.3 cm x .6 cm)

CUT

FOLD

CUT

ELEVATORS
$\frac{1}{2}$ in x $\frac{1}{4}$ in
(2.5 cm x .6 cm)

STEP 5 In the locations shown, measure, cut, and fold the elevators.

GLUE

STEP 6 Glue folds only at the center of fuselage. Flip airplane over. Adjust shape so that when viewed from the back, the airplane makes a shallow upside-down W, as shown.

14

DECORATION

Use this pattern to decorate the Egret. As with all the decorative patterns in this book, you may copy the entire pattern, use only a portion of it, or invent your own. The photograph on p 12 shows suggestions for colors.

NOTE For all the planes, draw the patterns and apply the colors before the final assembly is completed.

16

BACKGROUND INFORMATION
This airplane is called the "Pelican" because it has a kink in the middle that makes it look like a fat pelican. It is a modified delta (triangle) wing airplane and has a gentle and smooth glide.

MAKING THE AIRPLANE

The first two steps in building this airplane are identical to Egret. But the kink in the middle makes the finished plane shorter. Notice that this plane requires no gluing. It also has no vertical tail. Hold it between thumb and forefinger, launching it gently straight ahead. In flight the wings should be level.

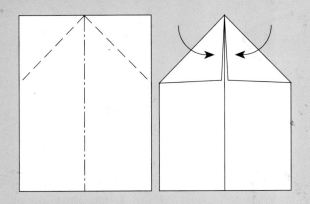

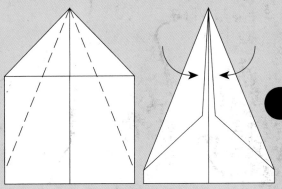

STEP 1 Lay the paper flat in a vertical direction. Fold paper in half vertically, using the mountain fold. Unfold. Then valley fold the upper corners to the center crease.

STEP 2 Valley fold the upper diagonals along broken lines to meet center crease.

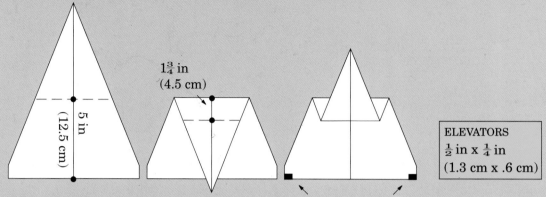

ELEVATORS
$\frac{1}{2}$ in x $\frac{1}{4}$ in
(1.3 cm x .6 cm)

$1\frac{3}{4}$ in
(4.5 cm)

5 in
(12.5 cm)

STEP 3 Flip airplane over. At the center crease, measure from bottom edge, as shown, and draw horizontal line. Valley fold along line. Then measure down from fold on center crease and draw another horizontal line. Valley fold along line bringing tip up. Make elevators in locations shown (see p 14).

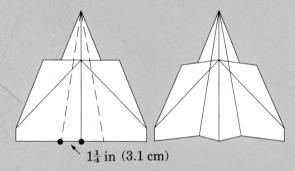

$1\frac{1}{4}$ in (3.1 cm)

STEP 4 Flip airplane over. Along bottom edge, measure, as shown, from each side of center crease and draw lines to upper tip. Valley fold along lines.

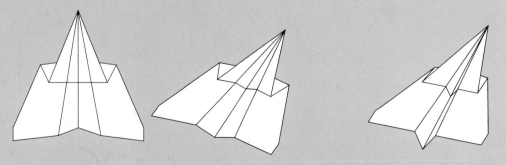

STEP 5 Flip airplane over. Adjust so that it forms a shallow upside-down W. In flight the wings should be level.

18

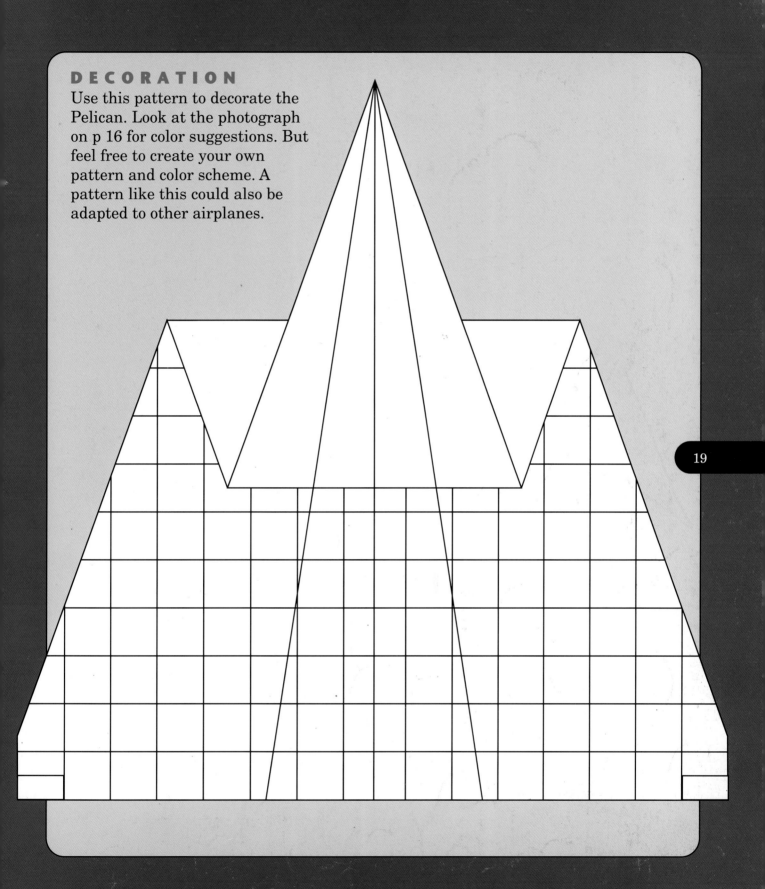

DECORATION

Use this pattern to decorate the Pelican. Look at the photograph on p 16 for color suggestions. But feel free to create your own pattern and color scheme. A pattern like this could also be adapted to other airplanes.

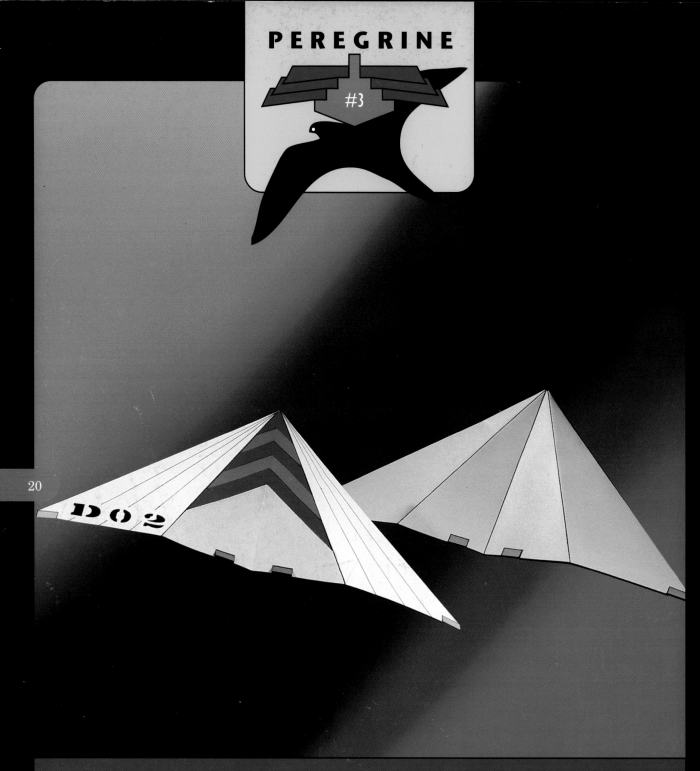

BACKGROUND INFORMATION

This airplane is called the "Peregrine" because of the way it soars in the breeze like a hawk when flown outdoors. In fact, the plane's wing span resembles that of the soaring hawk. This plane is called a flying wing because it has no fuselage and no tail surfaces. It is a very efficient design with low drag, but it is sensitive to trim. The flying wing design has been used in gliders as well as in heavy bombers, such as the Northrop B-2.

MAKING THE AIRPLANE

The flying wing is an interesting airplane design. It flies well outdoors when it is in proper trim. When trimming, be sure to get the bends in the wings to the proper angles. Experiment to adjust the airplane. Launch it straight ahead by holding it as shown on the next page. It needs only a gentle push, not a throw, to make it fly.

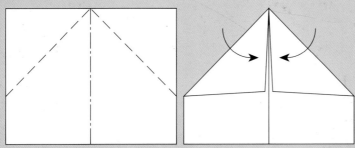

STEP 1 Lay the paper flat in a horizontal direction. Fold paper in half vertically, using a mountain fold. Unfold. Then valley fold the upper corners along broken lines to meet the center crease.

STEP 2 Valley fold upper tip to meet folded over corners at center crease.

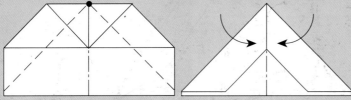

STEP 3 Valley fold diagonally from upper center point so that upper edges meet the center crease.

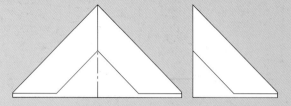

STEP 4 Fold airplane in half along the original mountain fold.

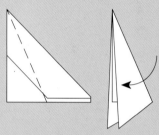

STEP 5 Valley fold each outer edge to meet center fold.

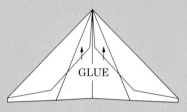

STEP 6 Unfold, as shown above. Flatten creases. Then glue the small triangles only.

AILERONS
ELEVATORS
$\frac{1}{2}$ in x $\frac{1}{4}$ in
(1.3 cm x .6 cm)

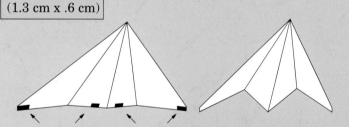

STEP 7 Flip airplane over. Viewed from the back, the wings form an upside down W. Make the control surfaces where shown (see p 14).

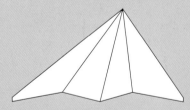

STEP 8 Adjust the W until you get the best glide. Trim with slight up elevator. To launch, hold as shown.

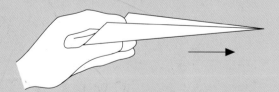

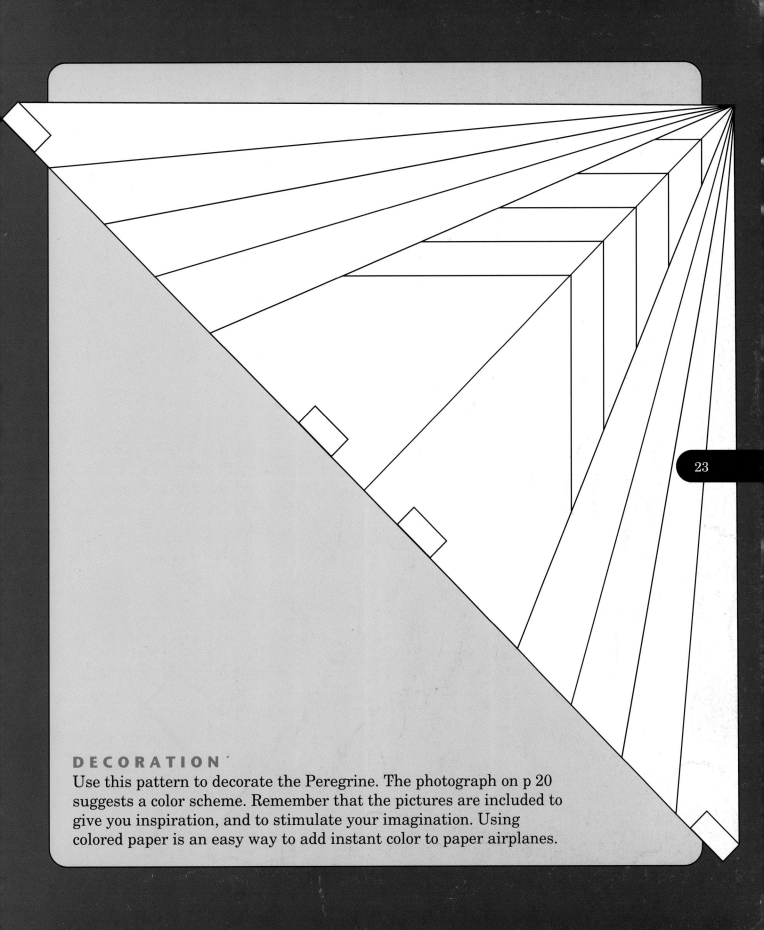

DECORATION

Use this pattern to decorate the Peregrine. The photograph on p 20 suggests a color scheme. Remember that the pictures are included to give you inspiration, and to stimulate your imagination. Using colored paper is an easy way to add instant color to paper airplanes.

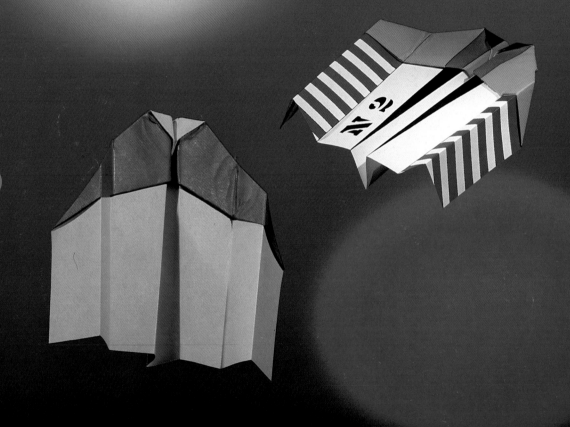

BACKGROUND INFORMATION
This airplane is called the "Pipit" because of its small size, just like the bird by that name. This paper airplane has small wings for its weight, which makes it a fast flyer. It can be thrown hard. It is well suited for flight both indoors and out.

MAKING THE AIRPLANE

The Pipit is a compact little airplane folded entirely from one sheet of paper. It can be constructed without control surfaces. For trimming adjustment, bend the entire airplane. If thrown hard, it will fly not only fast but far. For launching, hold it between thumb and forefinger.

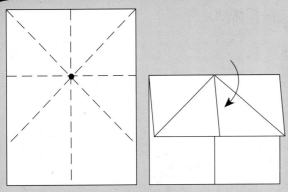

STEP 1 Lay paper flat in a vertical direction. Fold paper in half vertically using a valley fold. Unfold. Then valley fold diagonally so that right upper edge meets the left outer edge. Unfold. Repeat, folding down left upper edge. Unfold. Using the intersection of the creases as a reference, valley fold upper section of the paper, along broken horizontal line, as shown.

STEP 2 Unfold paper. Valley fold top edge to horizontal crease. Valley fold again along horizontal crease.

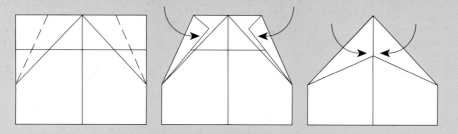

STEP 3 Using a valley fold, bring outer edge to meet the right diagonal crease. Repeat, folding over left edge. Then valley fold the diagonal creases.

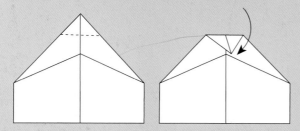

STEP 4 Valley fold tip down to meet crease, as shown.

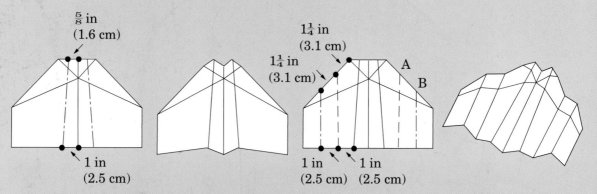

$\frac{5}{8}$ in
(1.6 cm)

1 in
(2.5 cm)

$1\frac{1}{4}$ in
(3.1 cm)

$1\frac{1}{4}$ in
(3.1 cm)

A

B

1 in
(2.5 cm)

1 in
(2.5 cm)

STEP 5 On each side of vertical center crease, measure and draw lines as indicated. Then mountain fold along drawn lines, as shown. Measure and draw the next two sets of lines, on each side. Valley fold line A and mountain fold line B on each side, as shown.

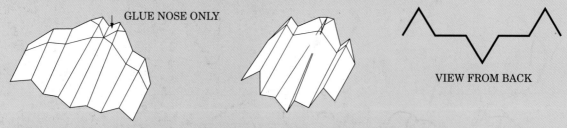

GLUE NOSE ONLY

VIEW FROM BACK

STEP 6 Glue nose only, let back flare open. Adjust so that, when viewed from back, it makes a shape as indicated.

DECORATION

Use this pattern to decorate the Pipit.
Refer to the photograph on p 24 for
color suggestions. Does the shape of
the airplane suggest a different
pattern to you? Be creative and invent
your own.

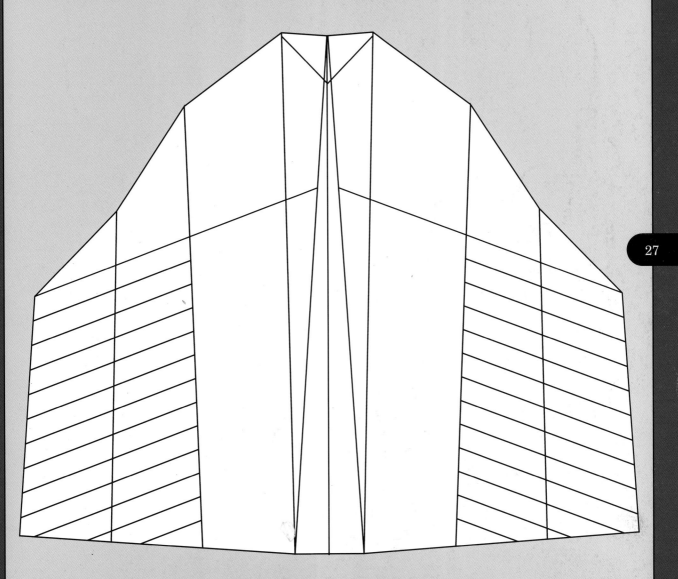

COOT

#5

BACKGROUND INFORMATION

This airplane is called the "Coot" because it is designed with a heavy body. It resembles the stubby body and short wings of the duck-like bird of the same name. This airplane is a modified delta (triangle) wing design. It is shaped like some of today's fighter planes, such as the Grumman F14, when it is in high-speed trim.

MAKING THE AIRPLANE

The Coot is similar in construction to the Pelican, but it is slightly more complicated to finish. It is designed with a canopy for added realism. Make sure that its shape is properly adjusted, with no dihedral (upward slanting of wings) when in flight. Hold it between thumb and forefinger, launching it briskly straight ahead.

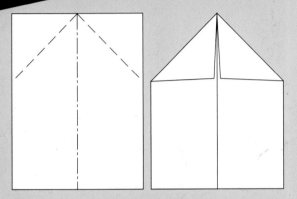

STEP 1 Lay the paper flat in a vertical direction. Fold paper in half vertically, using a mountain fold. Unfold. Then valley fold upper corners to the center crease.

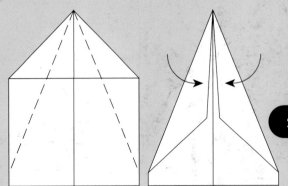

STEP 2 Valley fold upper diagonals along broken lines to meet center crease.

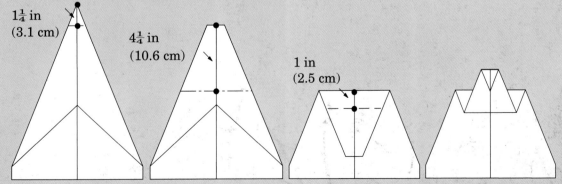

$1\frac{1}{4}$ in (3.1 cm)

$4\frac{1}{4}$ in (10.6 cm)

1 in (2.5 cm)

STEP 3 Measure down from tip along center crease, as shown, and make a mountain fold. Measure from fold along center crease, as shown, and mountain fold again. Flip airplane over. From fold, measure down along center crease and valley fold, as shown.

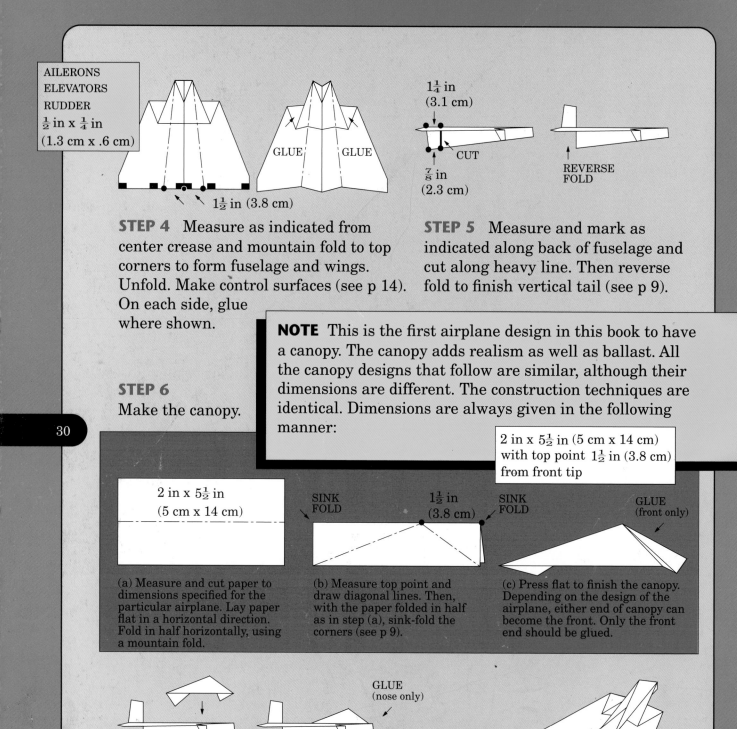

AILERONS
ELEVATORS
RUDDER
$\frac{1}{2}$ in x $\frac{1}{4}$ in
(1.3 cm x .6 cm)

GLUE   GLUE

$1\frac{1}{2}$ in (3.8 cm)

$1\frac{1}{4}$ in
(3.1 cm)

CUT

$\frac{7}{8}$ in
(2.3 cm)

REVERSE
FOLD

STEP 4 Measure as indicated from center crease and mountain fold to top corners to form fuselage and wings. Unfold. Make control surfaces (see p 14). On each side, glue where shown.

STEP 5 Measure and mark as indicated along back of fuselage and cut along heavy line. Then reverse fold to finish vertical tail (see p 9).

NOTE This is the first airplane design in this book to have a canopy. The canopy adds realism as well as ballast. All the canopy designs that follow are similar, although their dimensions are different. The construction techniques are identical. Dimensions are always given in the following manner:

2 in x $5\frac{1}{2}$ in (5 cm x 14 cm) with top point $1\frac{1}{2}$ in (3.8 cm) from front tip

STEP 6
Make the canopy.

2 in x $5\frac{1}{2}$ in
(5 cm x 14 cm)

SINK
FOLD

$1\frac{1}{2}$ in
(3.8 cm)

SINK
FOLD

GLUE
(front only)

(a) Measure and cut paper to dimensions specified for the particular airplane. Lay paper flat in a horizontal direction. Fold in half horizontally, using a mountain fold.

(b) Measure top point and draw diagonal lines. Then, with the paper folded in half as in step (a), sink-fold the corners (see p 9).

(c) Press flat to finish the canopy. Depending on the design of the airplane, either end of canopy can become the front. Only the front end should be glued.

GLUE
(nose only)

STEP 7 Insert canopy into fuselage to align with nose. Glue in place, applying glue only to the inside nose area of fuselage and the small triangle of the canopy. Leave the back to flare open. Wings should have no dihedral.

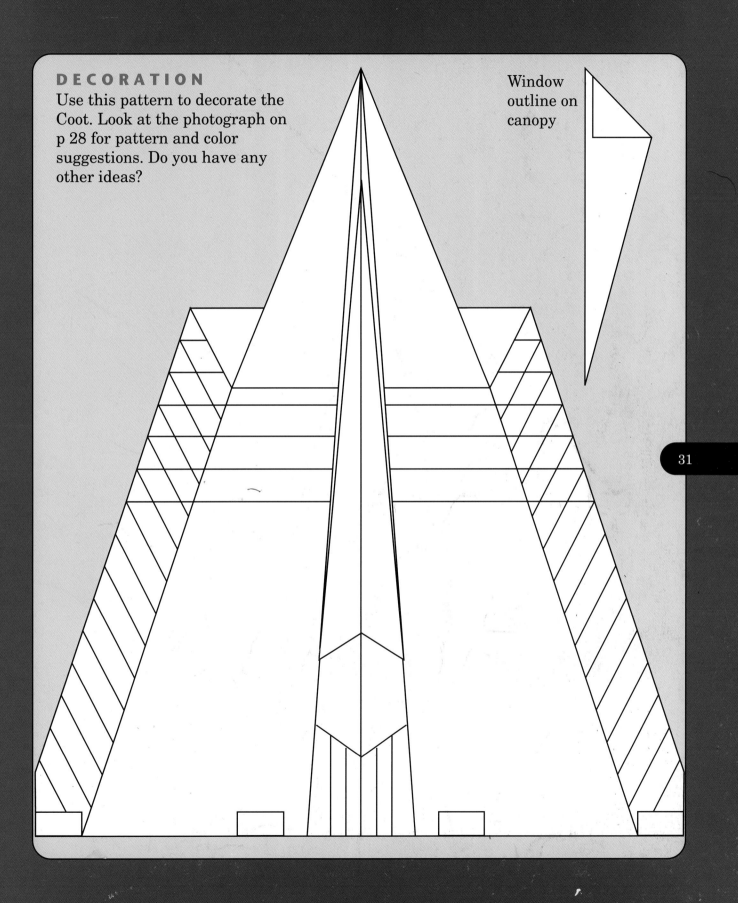

DECORATION
Use this pattern to decorate the
Coot. Look at the photograph on
p 28 for pattern and color
suggestions. Do you have any
other ideas?

Window
outline on
canopy

BACKGROUND INFORMATION

This airplane is called the "Swallow" because of its deeply forked tail which resembles that of the bird. When airplanes where first invented, many different kinds of tails where tried. This is an interesting looking airplane. It can soar in a gentle breeze.

MAKING THE AIRPLANE

The Swallow is also folded completely from one sheet of paper. It can be constructed without control surfaces. For trimming adjustment, bend the entire airplane. For launching, hold between thumb and forefinger. Launch this airplane gently. Fly it indoors or out.

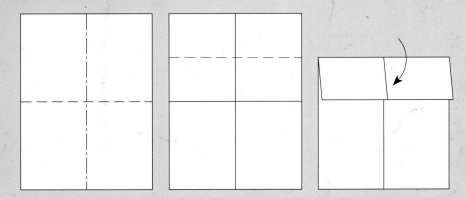

STEP 1 Lay paper flat in a vertical direction. Fold paper in half vertically using a mountain fold. Unfold. Valley fold the paper in half horizontally. Unfold. Then valley fold the top to meet the horizontal crease.

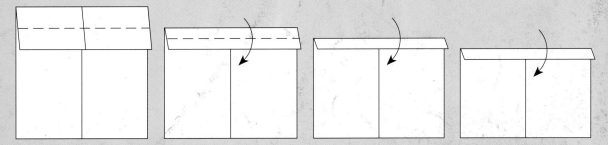

STEP 2 Valley fold the top again to meet the horizontal crease. Then valley fold top again, to meet the horizontal crease. Finally, refold the original horizontal crease.

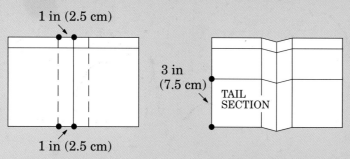

1 in (2.5 cm)

1 in (2.5 cm)

3 in (7.5 cm)

TAIL SECTION

STEP 3 On each side, measure from center crease and draw lines, as shown. Valley fold along these lines. Unfold. Measure from bottom along side and draw a horizontal line.

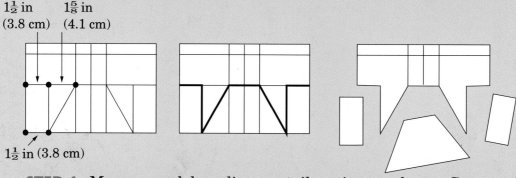

$1\frac{1}{2}$ in (3.8 cm)

$1\frac{5}{8}$ in (4.1 cm)

$1\frac{1}{2}$ in (3.8 cm)

STEP 4 Measure and draw lines on tail section, as shown. Cut out along heavy lines, as shown. Discard cutouts.

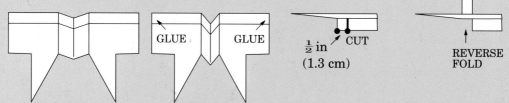

GLUE   GLUE

$\frac{1}{2}$ in (1.3 cm)   CUT

REVERSE FOLD

STEP 5 Reshape the airplane by refolding the vertical creases. At each wingtip, glue folded-over portion of the wing's leading (front) edge. Glue no more than 1 in (2.5 cm) from each wingtip.

STEP 6 Measure, draw, and cut along heavy line at back of fuselage, as shown. Reverse fold to make the vertical tail (see p 9).

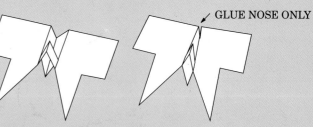

GLUE NOSE ONLY

STEP 7 Apply glue to the nose only, leaving the back to flare open. Adjust the wings so they are level in flight.

DECORATION

Use this pattern to decorate the Swallow.
The photograph on p 32 suggests a color
scheme. Do you have any other ideas?

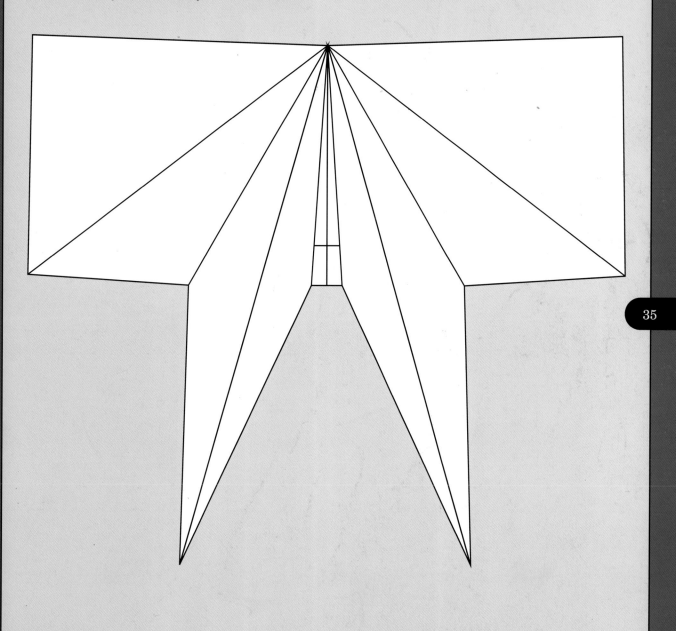

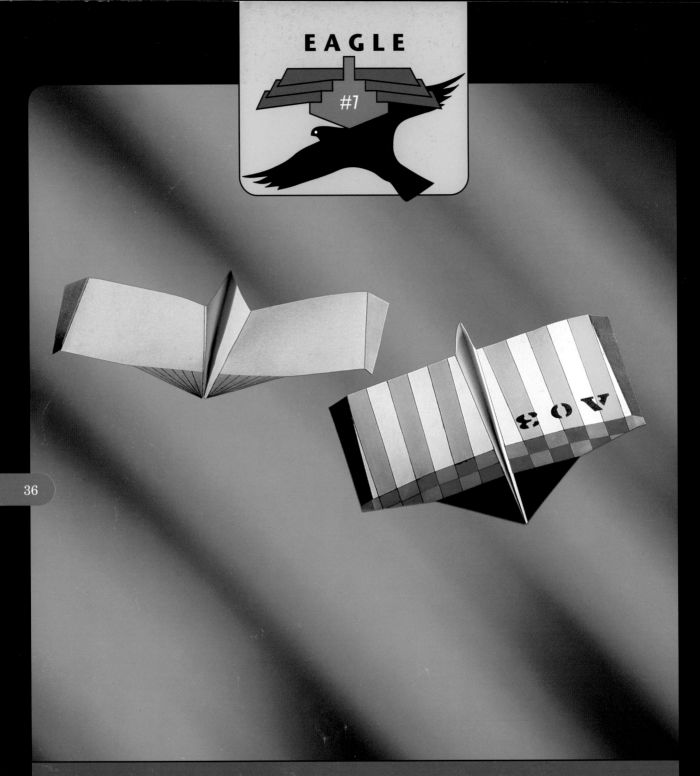

BACKGROUND INFORMATION

This airplane is named the "Eagle" because, like the bird, it can soar on the wind. This is because the airplane has large wings for its weight, which makes it slow but very buoyant. Try trimming this plane for flight when the wind is brisk.

MAKING THE AIRPLANE

This airplane soars well, both indoors and out. It can be built without control surfaces and trimmed simply by bending the winglets. The flatter the winglets, the less nose-up the trim.

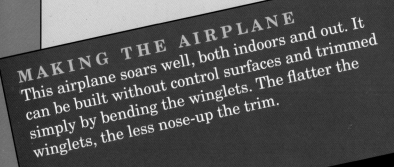

$2\frac{1}{2}$ in (6.3 cm)

STEP 1 Lay paper flat in a vertical direction. Measure as shown and draw a horizontal line. Valley fold along line. Then unfold. Valley fold top edge to crease. Valley fold again along original crease.

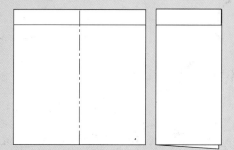

STEP 2 Mountain fold paper in half vertically.

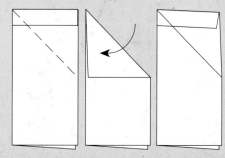

STEP 3 Valley fold top layer of paper diagonally so that top outer corner meets center crease. Then unfold. Turn over and repeat for other side of plane. Unfold diagonal creases.

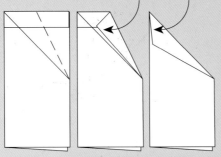

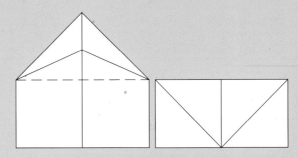

STEP 4 Valley fold top layer diagonally so that top outer corner meets the previous diagonal crease. Then refold previous diagonal. Turn over and repeat for other side of plane.

STEP 5 Unfold center fold. Then valley fold as indicated by broken line so that tip meets bottom center.

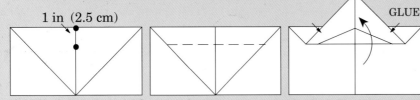

1 in (2.5 cm)

GLUE

STEP 6 Measure down from the top fold, as shown, and draw horizontal line. Valley fold along this line so that the tip is back at the top. Glue wings.

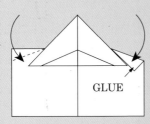

GLUE

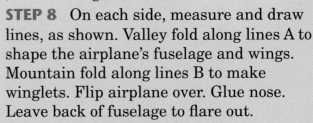

$\frac{1}{2}$ in (1.3 cm)

A

B

$\frac{1}{4}$ in (.6 cm)

1 in (2.5 cm)

$\frac{1}{2}$ in (1.3 cm)

GLUE NOSE ONLY

STEP 7 At the wing tips, make a valley fold along broken lines so that the top edges lie along the diagonals. Glue the small triangles.

STEP 8 On each side, measure and draw lines, as shown. Valley fold along lines A to shape the airplane's fuselage and wings. Mountain fold along lines B to make winglets. Flip airplane over. Glue nose. Leave back of fuselage to flare out.

STEP 9 Adjust dihedral (upward slanting of wings) so that airplane has this shape in flight (as viewed from the back).

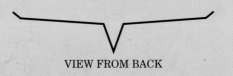

VIEW FROM BACK

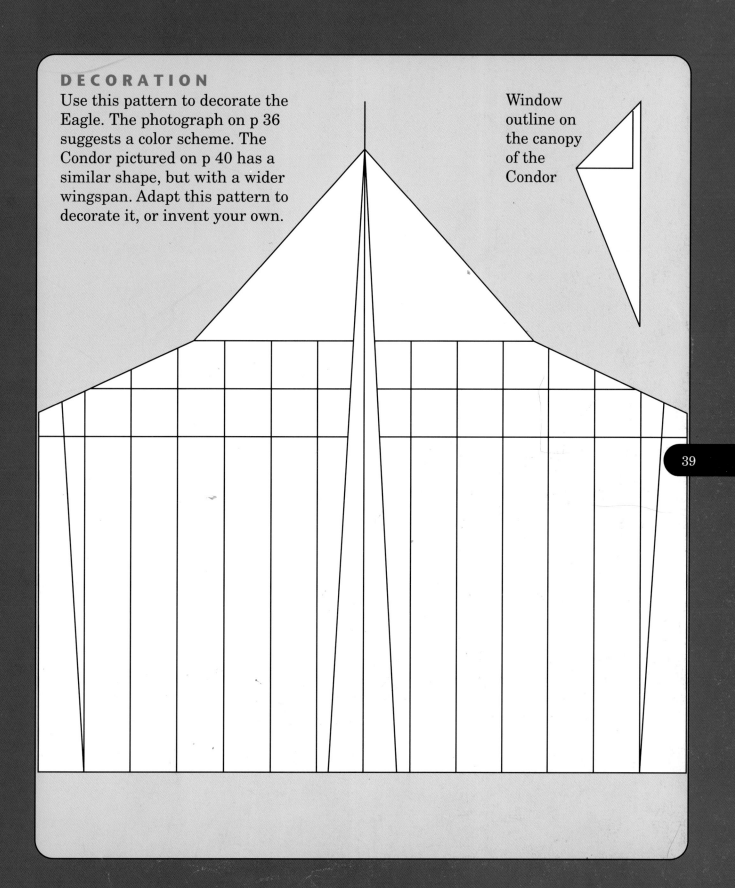

DECORATION

Use this pattern to decorate the Eagle. The photograph on p 36 suggests a color scheme. The Condor pictured on p 40 has a similar shape, but with a wider wingspan. Adapt this pattern to decorate it, or invent your own.

Window outline on the canopy of the Condor

CONDOR

#8

BACKGROUND INFORMATION

This airplane is called the "Condor" because of its large broad wings. This design is a variation on a flying wing. Unlike conventional airplanes, this design has no horizontal and vertical tail. Winglets are incorporated into the wing tips, which provide both horizontal and vertical stability. Like all flying wings, it is sensitive to pitch control. The wide wing span makes it quite fragile, and it should be launched gently straight ahead. It is not a windy weather airplane.

MAKING THE AIRPLANE

Condors have large feathers at their wingtips for control. Instead of feathers, this airplane has winglets. Because of its wide wing span, this paper airplane is fragile where the wings meet the fuselage. Adjust the winglets and bend the airplane for trim adjustment.

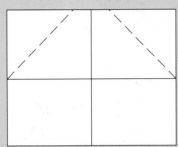

STEP 1 Lay paper flat in a horizontal direction. Fold paper in half vertically using the mountain fold. Unfold. Then valley fold in half horizontally. Unfold.

STEP 2 On each side, valley fold diagonally so that the outer edges meet the horizontal crease.

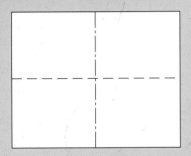

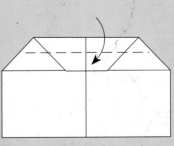

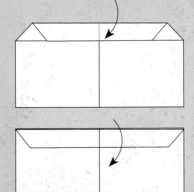

STEP 3 Valley fold along broken lines so that top edge meets the horizontal crease. Valley fold again, so that top edge meets the horizontal crease. Then refold the original horizontal crease.

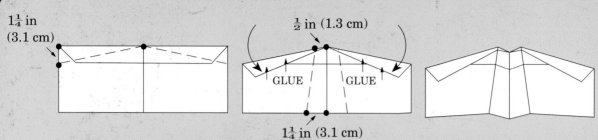

$1\frac{1}{4}$ in
(3.1 cm)

$\frac{1}{2}$ in (1.3 cm)

GLUE   GLUE

$1\frac{1}{4}$ in (3.1 cm)

STEP 4 On each side of vertical crease, measure and draw diagonal lines. Valley fold top outer edges along these lines. Glue folded over triangles to form the leading (front) edges of the wings. Then measure and draw vertical lines, as shown. Valley fold along vertical lines to form the fuselage.

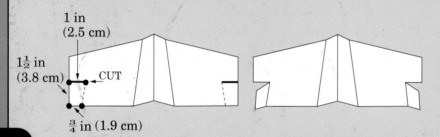

1 in
(2.5 cm)

$1\frac{1}{2}$ in
(3.8 cm)

CUT

$\frac{3}{4}$ in (1.9 cm)

STANDARD CANOPY
2 in x 3 in (5 cm x 7.5 cm)
with top point $1\frac{1}{4}$ in (3.1 cm)
from front tip

STEP 5 Flip the airplane over. On each side, measure and draw lines for the winglets. Make horizontal cuts on heavy lines. Valley fold, as indicated, to make winglets. Make a standard canopy (see p 30).

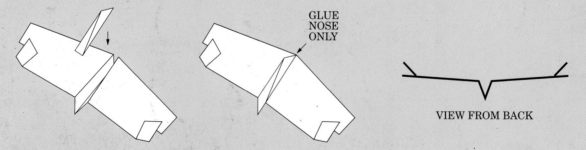

GLUE
NOSE
ONLY

VIEW FROM BACK

STEP 6 Apply glue to inside of nose only, and insert canopy. Align with nose. Adjust the shape so that the wings have a slight dihedral angle (upward slant) and the winglets slant upward, as shown.

42

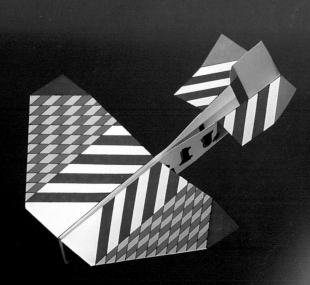

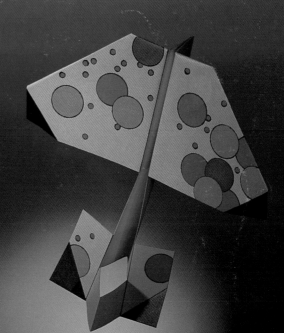

BACKGROUND INFORMATION

This airplane is designed to fly stunts. It is called the "Mockingbird" because it's a teaser. It won't fly straight. From the very beginning of aeronautics, pilots have tested their flying skills by doing stunts — aerobatic maneuvers such as loops, rolls, spins, and tumbles. Today pilots demonstrate maneuvers at air shows. Several airplanes, such as the Pitts Special and the Sukhoi 26, are made specifically for aerobatics. They are small in size with large control surfaces, making them highly maneuverable. To make them more visible, they are decorated in bold patterns and painted in bright colors.

44

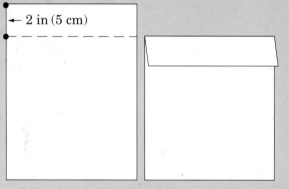

← 2 in (5 cm)

STEP 1 Lay the paper flat in a vertical direction. Measure down from the top and draw line. Valley fold along this line.

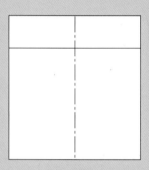

STEP 2 Mountain fold paper in half vertically. Unfold.

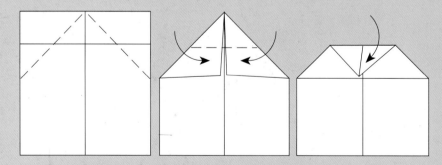

STEP 3 Fold top outer corners diagonally to meet the center crease, using a valley fold. Then valley fold upper tip to meet folded edges along center crease.

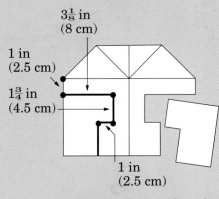

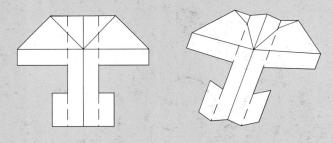

STEP 4 On each side, measure, cut, and discard paper, as shown.

STEP 5 Valley fold outer edges of wings and horizontal tail along inner cut lines, indicated by broken lines.

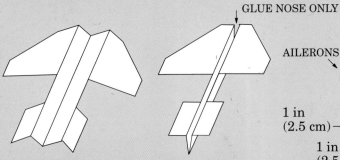

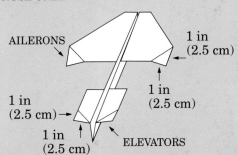

STEP 6 Flip airplane over. Adjust folds to form the airplane, as shown. Glue nose only. The back of the fuselage is left to flare open.

STEP 7 On each corner, measure and draw diagonals for control surfaces. Bend ailerons down and elevators up.

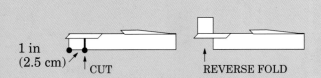

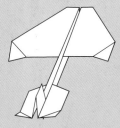

STEP 8 Measure, cut, and reverse fold, popping up the vertical tail (see p 9). Adjust folds so that in flight the wings have slight dihedral (upward slanting) and the horizontal tail has anhedral (downward slanting).

DECORATION

Use this pattern to decorate the Mockingbird. The photograph on p 43 suggests a color scheme. It also shows a second pattern, which is made by tracing around coins. Use bright colors for this aerobatic airplane.

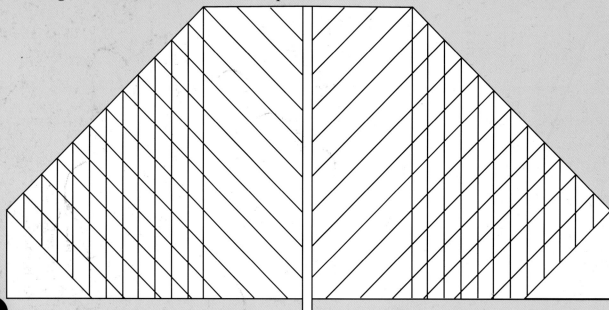

BACKGROUND INFORMATION

This airplane is called the "Thrush" because of its slender shape and pointed nose that resembles the slim body and long beak of the bird. It is a modified delta wing design (triangle). Its twin vertical tails are amid-ship, like those on the McDonnell Douglas F18.

MAKING THE AIRPLANE

The Thrush is constructed similarily to the Mockingbird, but it is a very different sort of aircraft. Hold it between thumb and forefinger, launching it straight ahead. This paper airplane performs well indoors and out, even in brisk wind.

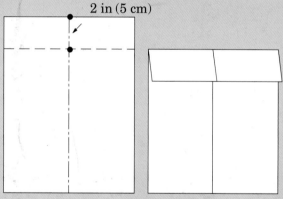

2 in (5 cm)

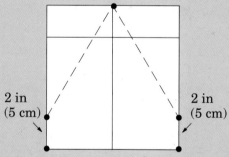

2 in (5 cm)   2 in (5 cm)

STEP 1 Lay paper flat in a vertical direction. Fold paper in half vertically using a mountain fold. Unfold. Then measure down from top along center fold and draw a line. Valley fold on this line.

STEP 2 Measure and draw lines, as shown. Valley fold along these lines. Unfold.

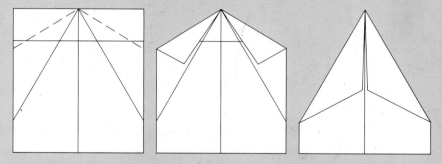

STEP 3 On each side, valley fold so that upper edge meets diagonal crease. Refold original diagonal creases.

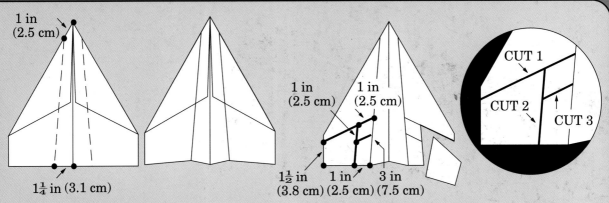

STEP 4 On each side of center crease, measure and draw lines as indicated. Valley fold along these lines. Unfold.

STEP 5 Flip airplane over. On each side, measure and draw lines, as shown. Cut along these lines (see inset), and discard paper.

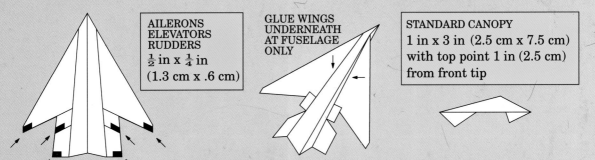

AILERONS
ELEVATORS
RUDDERS
$\frac{1}{2}$ in x $\frac{1}{4}$ in
(1.3 cm x .6 cm)

GLUE WINGS
UNDERNEATH
AT FUSELAGE
ONLY

STANDARD CANOPY
1 in x 3 in (2.5 cm x 7.5 cm)
with top point 1 in (2.5 cm)
from front tip

STEP 6 Make the control surfaces (see p 14). Adjust folds to form the airplane, as shown. From underneath, glue wings at fuselage only.

STEP 7 Make a standard canopy. (See p 30.)

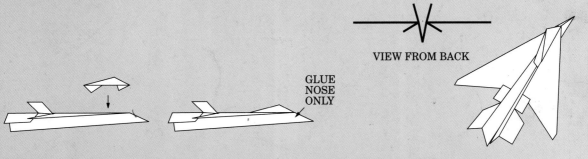

VIEW FROM BACK

GLUE
NOSE
ONLY

STEP 8 Insert canopy into fuselage so that front diagonal edges align. Apply glue only to small triangle of the canopy and the front of the fuselage, allowing the back to flare open. Adjust the wings to have no dihedral (upward slanting). The vertical tails should be almost vertical, and the horizontal tail should have anhedral (downward slanting).

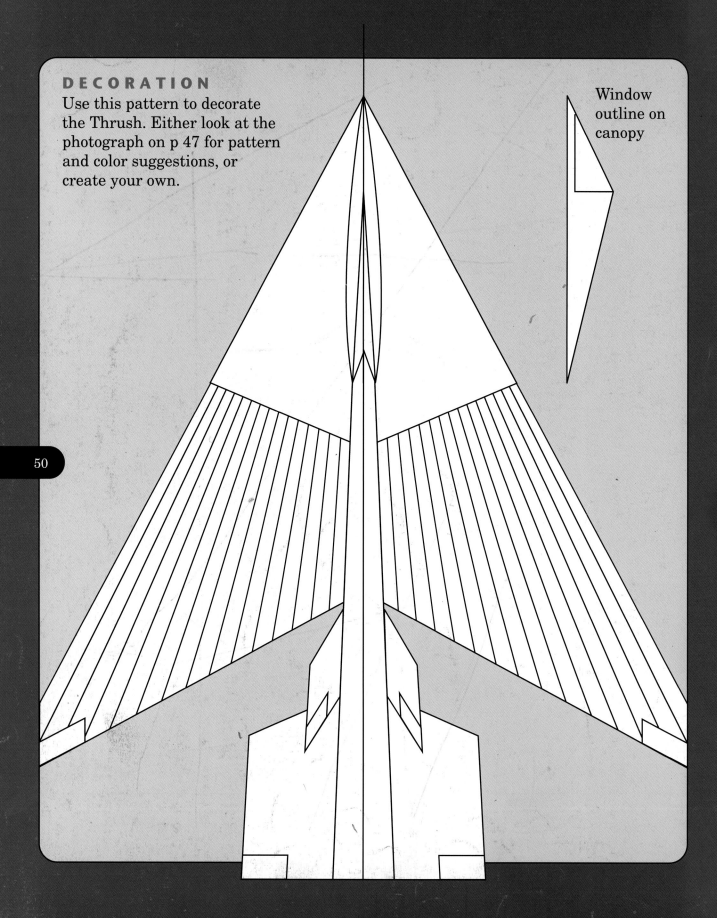

DECORATION
Use this pattern to decorate
the Thrush. Either look at the
photograph on p 47 for pattern
and color suggestions, or
create your own.

Window
outline on
canopy

50

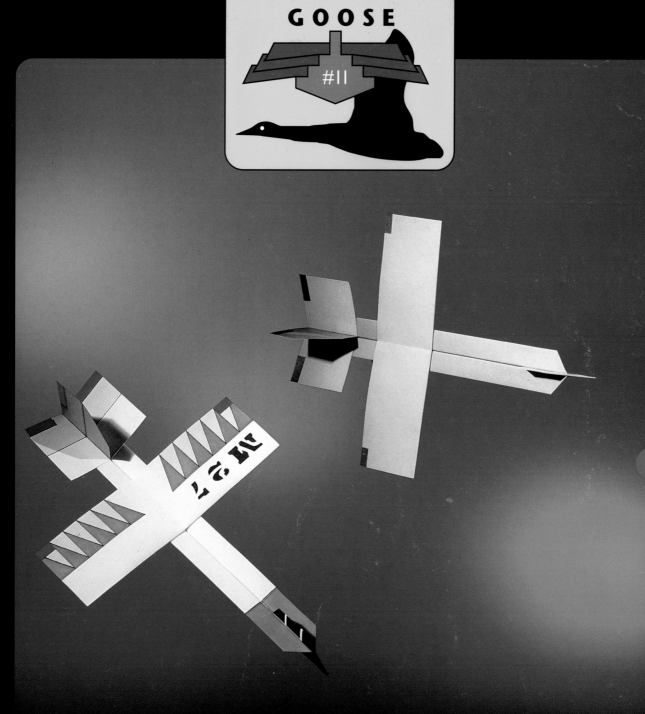

GOOSE

#11

BACKGROUND INFORMATION

This airplane is called the "Goose" because of its long fuselage protruding in front of the wings. It looks like a goose in flight. Many airplanes built today have their wings placed quite far back, allowing for more cargo and passenger space ahead of the wings, where the weight has to be concentrated, such as the Douglas DC9. This paper airplane is modeled on this aircraft design.

MAKING THE AIRPLANE

This is a conventional airplane design, having a fuselage, wings, and a tail with one vertical and two horizontal surfaces. Most real airplanes are built utilizing this general design. The Goose is the first of a number of paper airplanes in this book that follow similar building techniques. To fly, launch, holding it between thumb and forefinger.

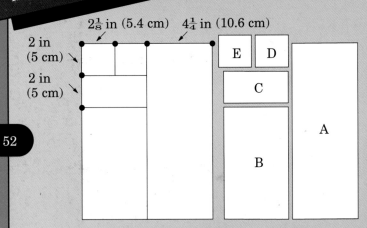

$2\frac{1}{8}$ in (5.4 cm) $4\frac{1}{4}$ in (10.6 cm)

2 in (5 cm)

2 in (5 cm)

STEP 1 Measure and cut out the various pieces from a sheet of bond paper, as shown.

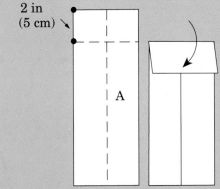

2 in (5 cm)

STEP 2 To make the fuselage, fold piece A in half vertically using a valley fold. Unfold. Measure from top, draw a horizontal line, as shown, and valley fold.

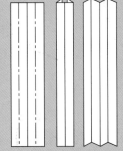

VIEW FROM BACK
(actual size)

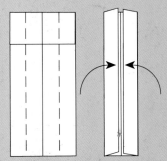

STEP 3 Valley fold each side so that outer edges meet center crease, as shown.

STEP 4 Fold again using a mountain fold, so that outer edges meet center crease at back. Then adjust folds so that paper looks like an upside-down W, as shown.

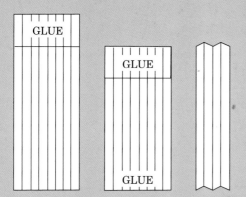

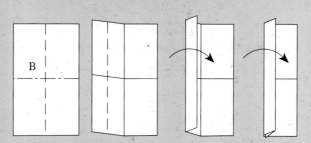

STEP 5 Unfold fuselage completely. Refold applying glue to contacting surfaces, as shown. Make sure fuselage is straight. Set aside.

STEP 6 Use piece B to make the wings. Fold in half vertically, using a valley fold. Unfold. Fold in half horizontally using a mountain fold. Unfold. Then valley fold vertically so that outer edge meets center crease. Fold over again along vertical center crease.

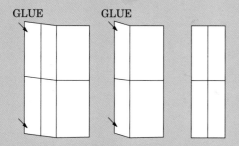

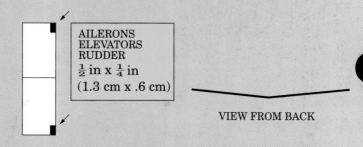

AILERONS
ELEVATORS
RUDDER
$\frac{1}{2}$ in x $\frac{1}{4}$ in
(1.3 cm x .6 cm)

VIEW FROM BACK

STEP 7 Unfold completely. Refold, applying glue to no more than 1 in (2.5 cm) from outer tips, as shown.

STEP 8 The folded over part is the bottom of the leading edge (front) of the wings. Make ailerons on trailing edges (back) in positions shown (see p 14). Adjust dihedral (upward slanting of wings), as shown.

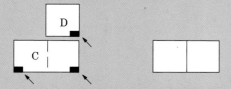

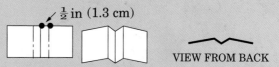

$\frac{1}{2}$ in (1.3 cm)

VIEW FROM BACK

STEP 9 Use pieces C and D to make the tail. First make the rudder and elevators on the trailing edges (back) (see p 14). Then fold piece C in half vertically, using a valley fold. Unfold.

STEP 10 On each side, measure from center crease and draw lines, as shown. Then mountain fold along lines. Viewed from back, piece should make an inverted W.

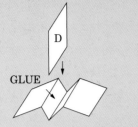

STEP 11 Join C and D to complete tail. Apply glue, sliding D into center section. Make sure rudder and elevators face the same direction.

VIEW FROM BACK

STEP 12 Use piece E to make the nose. Fold in half vertically using a valley fold and glue together.

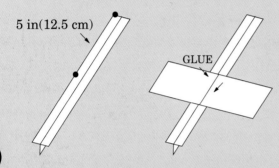

5 in(12.5 cm)

GLUE

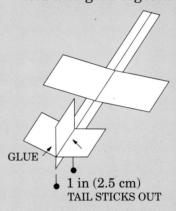

GLUE

1 in (2.5 cm)
TAIL STICKS OUT

STEP 13 Measure along front of fuselage and mark leading edge (front) position of wings. Glue wings in place, making sure that folded-over part is front bottom, and that the wings are centered and at right angles to fuselage.

STEP 14 Measure and mark along bottom of tail. Apply glue and slide tail into back of fuselage to the mark. Make sure control surfaces are at the back.

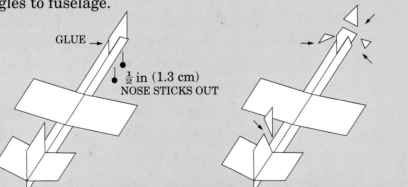

GLUE

$\frac{1}{2}$ in (1.3 cm)
NOSE STICKS OUT

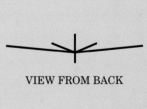

VIEW FROM BACK

STEP 15 Measure and mark bottom of nose. Apply glue and slide nose into front of fuselage to the mark.

STEP 16 Snip off the fronts of the nose and vertical tail at a slant, to finish the plane. Make sure that the dihedral angles (upward slanting) of wings and horizontal tail are as shown.

DECORATION

The pattern on this page can be used to
decorate the Goose. Because this airplane
is assembled using various pieces of paper,
it is easy to color it by making the wings,
horizontal tail, and vertical tail, using
paper of different colors (see p 51).

Window
outline on
canopy

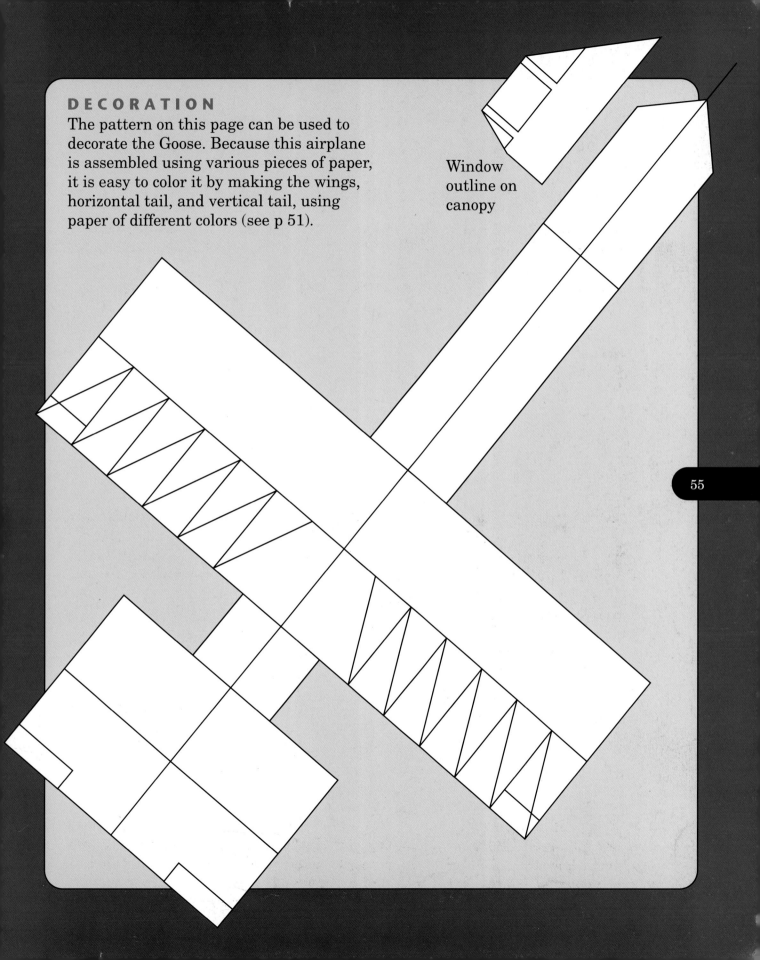

MERGANSER

#12

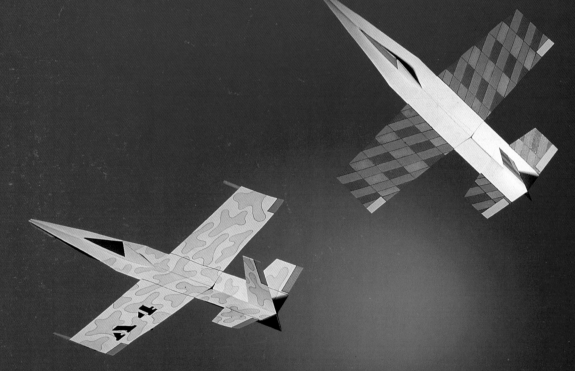

BACKGROUND INFORMATION

This airplane is called the "Merganser" because of its slender fuselage which resembles the slender body of the bird. This paper airplane is modeled on fighter planes of conventional design with straight tapered wings, such as the Canadair CL114 Tutor, the Lockheed T33, and the Lockheed F104.

The construction of this, and the next three airplanes, is similar to the Goose, but more complicated. When carefully made, these airplanes will go fast and far. They are maneuverable and can be trimmed for flying straight or for aerobatics, both indoors and out. Launch by holding between thumb and forefinger.

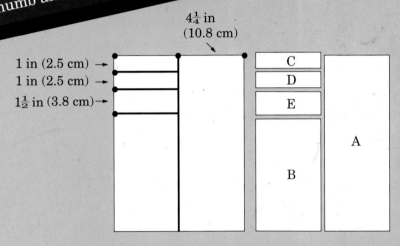

$4\frac{1}{4}$ in (10.8 cm)

1 in (2.5 cm) →
1 in (2.5 cm) →
$1\frac{1}{2}$ in (3.8 cm) →

C
D
E
A
B

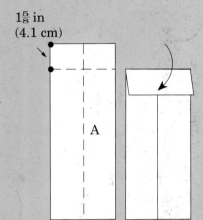

$1\frac{5}{8}$ in (4.1 cm)

A

STEP 1 Measure and cut the various pieces from a sheet of bond paper.

STEP 2 To make the fuselage, fold piece A in half vertically using a valley fold. Unfold. Measure from top and valley fold, as shown.

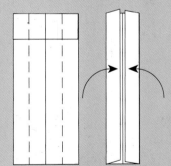

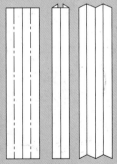

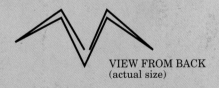

VIEW FROM BACK
(actual size)

STEP 3 Valley fold each side so that outer edges meet center crease, as shown.

STEP 4 Fold each side again using a mountain fold, so that outer edges meet center crease at back. Then adjust folds so that paper looks like an upside-down W, as shown.

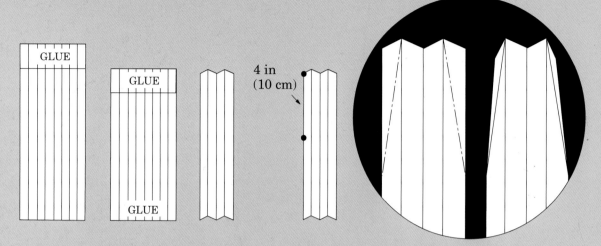

STEP 5 Unfold fuselage completely. Refold applying glue to contacting surfaces, as shown. Make sure fuselage is straight.

STEP 6 On each side, measure from top (front of fuselage), mark, and mountain fold, as shown in enlarged view.

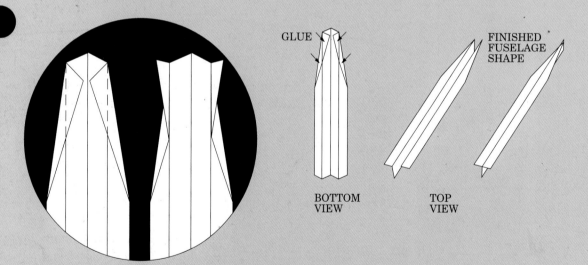

STEP 7 Flip over fuselage. On each side, valley fold triangle along broken lines, matching fold line to existing crease.

STEP 8 Glue triangles. Hold in place until glue sets. It is important that the fuselage stays straight. Do not glue nose yet.

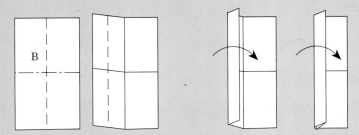

STEP 9 Use piece B to make the wings. Fold in half vertically, using a valley fold. Unfold. Fold in half horizontally using a mountain fold. Unfold. Then valley fold left side vertically so that one outer edge meets center crease. Fold over again along original vertical center crease.

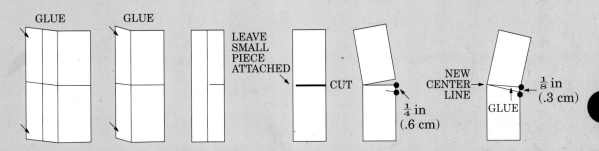

STEP 10 Unfold completely. Refold, applying glue to no more than 1 in (2.5 cm) from outer tips, as shown. The folded over part is the bottom of the leading edge (front) of the wings.

STEP 11 To taper wings, cut along center line from the trailing edge (back), leaving a small piece attached at the leading edge. Then measure and make a mark on trailing edge, as shown. Align pieces to the mark. Glue. Measure and draw a new center line.

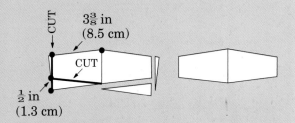

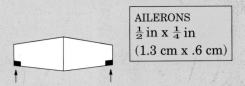

STEP 12 To finish tapered wings, measure, draw, and cut wingtips and trailing edges along heavy lines, as indicated.

STEP 13 On the trailing (back) edges, make ailerons (see p 14).

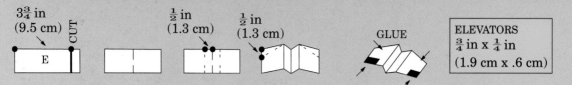

ELEVATORS
$\frac{3}{4}$ in x $\frac{1}{4}$ in
(1.9 cm x .6 cm)

STEP 14 Use piece E to make the horizontal tail. Cut to dimensions indicated. Valley fold in half vertically. Unfold. On each side, measure from center crease, as shown, and mountain fold. On each side, measure and mountain fold leading edge along broken lines. Glue. Make elevators on trailing edges (see p 14).

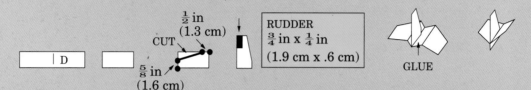

RUDDER
$\frac{3}{4}$ in x $\frac{1}{4}$ in
(1.9 cm x .6 cm)

STEP 15 Use piece D to make the vertical tail. Valley fold in half vertically and glue together. Then measure and cut along heavy line, as shown. Make rudder on trailing edge (see p 14).

STEP 16 Join pieces D and E to finish tail. Apply glue and slide D into center of E, aligning trailing edges.

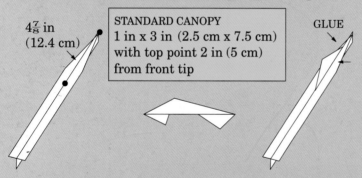

STANDARD CANOPY
1 in x 3 in (2.5 cm x 7.5 cm)
with top point 2 in (5 cm)
from front tip

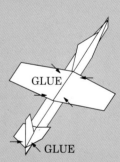

STEP 17 Use piece C to make standard canopy (see p 30). Measure from front of fuselage and mark. Use this dot for positioning back of canopy. Apply glue to inside of nose and the small triangles on the bottom of canopy. Hold until glue sets.

STEP 18 Use dot (back of canopy) for positioning leading edge of wings. Glue in place, making sure wings are centered and at right angles to the fuselage. Apply glue and slide tail into back of fuselage so that trailing edges align.

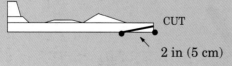

CUT
2 in (5 cm)

BACK VIEW

STEP 19 Measure and cut front of fuselage diagonally along heavy line to finish nose.

STEP 20 Adjust dihedral (upward slanting) of wings and horizontal tail, as shown.

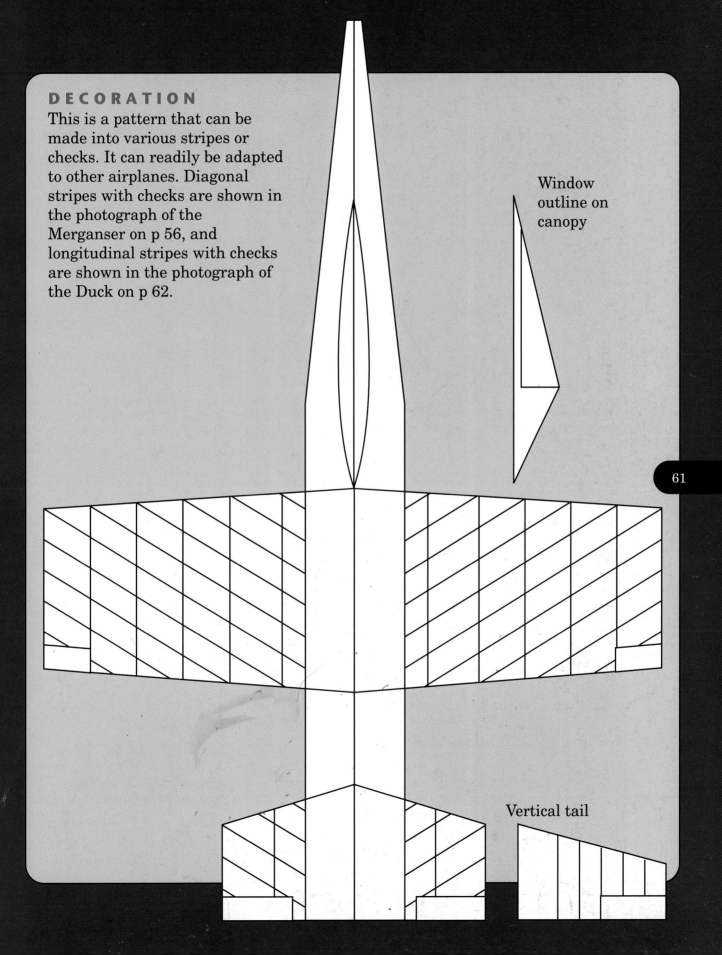

DECORATION

This is a pattern that can be made into various stripes or checks. It can readily be adapted to other airplanes. Diagonal stripes with checks are shown in the photograph of the Merganser on p 56, and longitudinal stripes with checks are shown in the photograph of the Duck on p 62.

Window outline on canopy

61

Vertical tail

DUCK

#13

BACKGROUND INFORMATION

This paper airplane is called the "Duck" because of its long slim shape. It is modeled on the airplane known as a "canard" which is French for duck. Canard airplanes have the wings positioned toward the back of the fuselage and the horizontal "tail" — known as canard wings — toward the front. The Beech Starship and the Saab 37 Viggen are examples of such a design.

MAKING THE AIRPLANE

When carefully made, this airplane is very stable in the air and has a flat glide. It will go fast and far. It can be trimmed to fly straight or it can be made to do aerobatics. Launch the plane by holding it between thumb and forefinger. Notice that in order to trim for nose up, the elevators must be bent down.

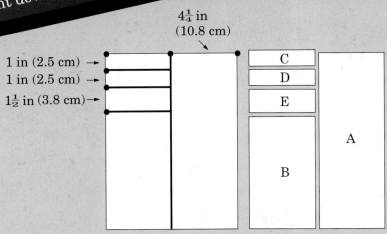

4¼ in (10.8 cm)

1 in (2.5 cm) →
1 in (2.5 cm) →
1½ in (3.8 cm) →

C
D
E
B
A

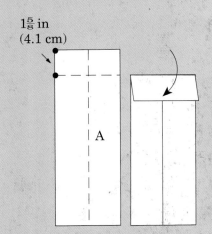

1⅝ in (4.1 cm)

A

STEP 1 Measure and cut the various pieces from a sheet of bond paper.

STEP 2 To make the fuselage, fold piece A in half vertically using a valley fold. Unfold. Measure from top and valley fold, as shown.

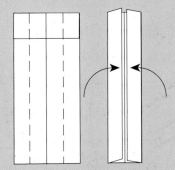

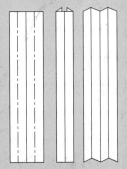

VIEW FROM BACK
(actual size)

STEP 3 Valley fold each side so that outer edges meet the center crease, as shown.

STEP 4 Fold each side again using a mountain fold, so that outer edges meet center crease at back. Then adjust folds so that paper looks like an upside-down W, as shown.

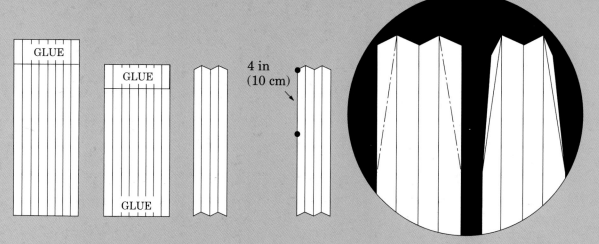

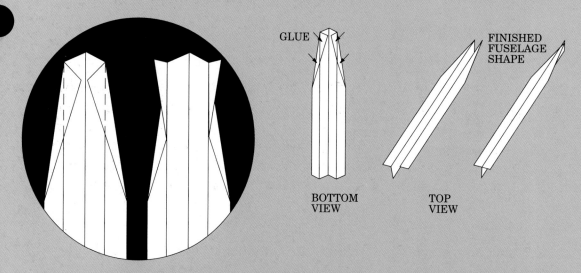

STEP 5 Unfold fuselage completely. Refold applying glue to contacting surfaces, as shown. Make sure fuselage is straight.

STEP 6 On each side, measure from top (front of fuselage), mark, and mountain fold along broken lines, as shown in enlarged view.

STEP 7 Flip over fuselage. On each side, valley fold triangle along broken lines, matching fold line to existing crease.

STEP 8 Glue triangles. Hold in place until glue sets. It is important that the fuselage stays straight. Do not glue nose yet.

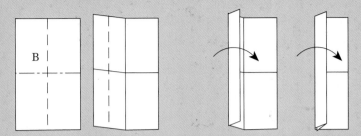

STEP 9 Use piece B to make the wings. Fold in half vertically, using a valley fold. Unfold. Fold in half horizontally using a mountain fold. Unfold. Then valley fold vertically so that one outer edge meets center crease. Fold over again along original vertical center crease.

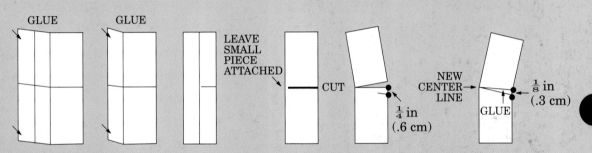

STEP 10 Unfold completely. Refold, applying glue to no more than 1 in (2.5 cm) from outer tips, as shown. The folded over part is the bottom of the leading edge (front) of the wings.

STEP 11 To taper wings, cut along center heavy line from the trailing (back) edge, leaving a small piece attached at the leading (front) edge. Then measure and make a mark on trailing edge, as shown. Align pieces to the mark. Glue. Measure and draw a new center line.

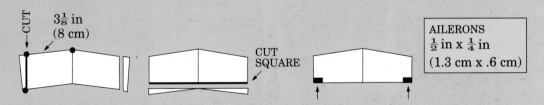

AILERONS
$\frac{1}{2}$ in x $\frac{1}{4}$ in
(1.3 cm x .6 cm)

STEP 12 To finish tapered wings, measure and cut wing tips along heavy lines. Then, using a ruler to mark, cut trailing edge square, as shown.

STEP 13 On the trailing edges, make ailerons (see p 14).

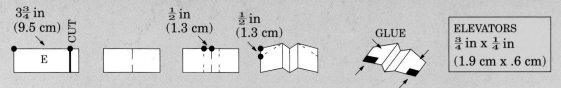

$3\frac{3}{4}$ in (9.5 cm) CUT E
$\frac{1}{2}$ in (1.3 cm)
$\frac{1}{2}$ in (1.3 cm)
GLUE

STEP 14 Use piece E to make the canard wing. Cut to dimensions indicated. Valley fold in half vertically. Unfold. On each side, measure from center crease, as shown, and mountain fold. On each side, measure and mountain fold leading edge along broken lines. Glue. Make elevators on trailing edges (see p 14).

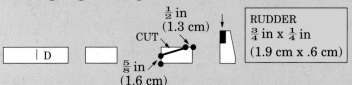

D CUT $\frac{1}{2}$ in (1.3 cm) $\frac{5}{8}$ in (1.6 cm)

RUDDER
$\frac{3}{4}$ in x $\frac{1}{4}$ in
(1.9 cm x .6 cm)

STANDARD CANOPY
1 in x 3 in (2.5 cm x 7.5 cm)
with top point 2 in (5 cm)
from front tip

STEP 15 Use piece D to make the vertical tail. Valley fold in half vertically and glue together. Then measure and cut along heavy line, as shown. Make rudder on trailing edge (see p 14).

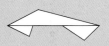

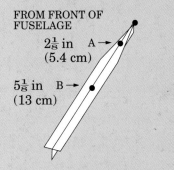

FROM FRONT OF FUSELAGE
$2\frac{1}{8}$ in (5.4 cm) A →
$5\frac{1}{8}$ in (13 cm) B →

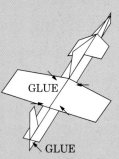

GLUE

GLUE

GLUE

STEP 16 Measure from front of fuselage, as shown, and make mark A for positioning leading edge of canard wings and front of canopy, and mark B for positioning leading edge of main wings.

STEP 17 Use piece C to make standard canopy (see p 30). Apply glue to inside of nose, the bottom of the canard wings, and the small triangles on the bottom of canopy. Slide in place together and hold until glue sets.

STEP 18 Glue main wings in place, with leading edge at mark B, making sure wings are centered and at right angles to the fuselage. Apply glue and slide vertical tail into back of fuselage so that trailing edges align.

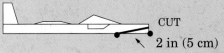
CUT
2 in (5 cm)

BACK VIEW

STEP 19 Measure and cut front of fuselage diagonally along heavy line to finish nose.

STEP 20 Adjust dihedral (upward slanting) of main wings and anhedral (downward slanting) of canard wings, as shown.

DECORATION

This is a military camouflage pattern. It can readily be adapted to other airplanes. The photographs show desert camouflage (p 56), forest camouflage (p 62), and sky camouflage (p 68). For military aircraft, toothpicks can be used to make antennae or armament.

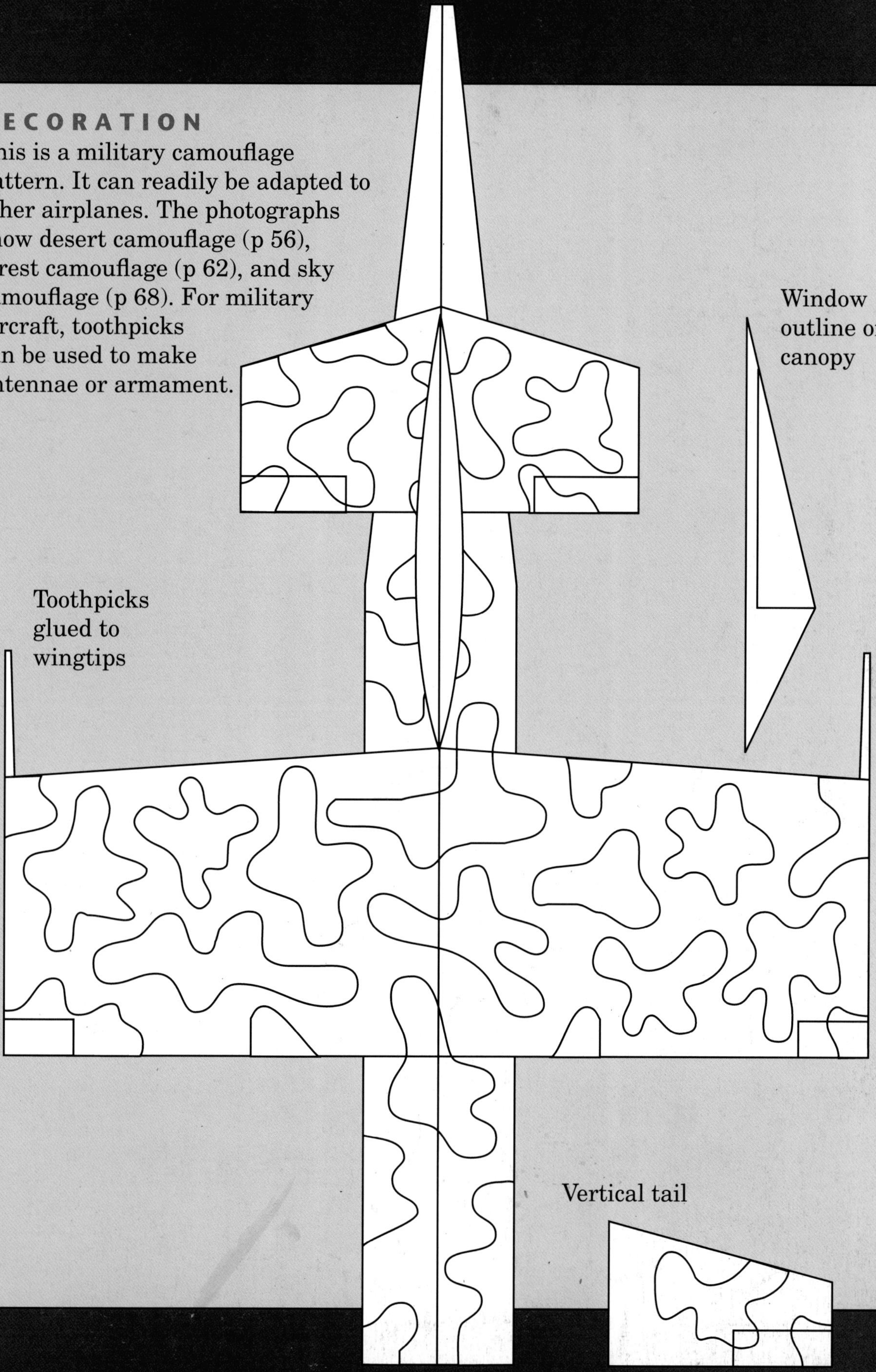

Window outline on canopy

Toothpicks glued to wingtips

Vertical tail

GREBE

#14

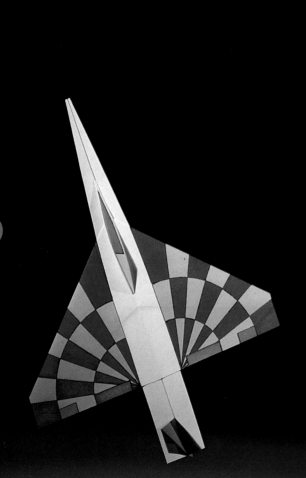

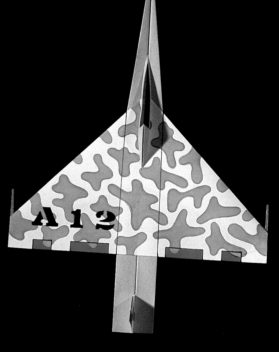

BACKGROUND INFORMATION

This paper airplane is called the "Grebe" because of its similarity to the duck-like grebe which has a very short tail and stubby wings. This paper airplane is a delta (triangle) wing airplane. It has no horizontal tail. It is modeled on delta wing fighter planes such as the General Dynamics F106 and the Dassault-Breguet Mirage 2000.

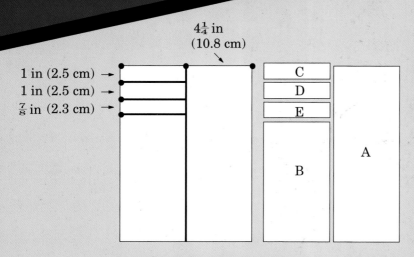

4¼ in
(10.8 cm)

1 in (2.5 cm) →
1 in (2.5 cm) →
⅞ in (2.3 cm) →

C
D
E
B
A

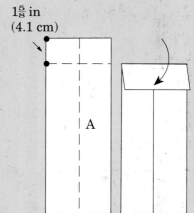

1⅝ in
(4.1 cm)

A

A

STEP 1 Measure and cut the various pieces from a sheet of bond paper.

STEP 2 To make the fuselage, fold piece A in half vertically using a valley fold. Unfold. Measure from top and valley fold, as shown.

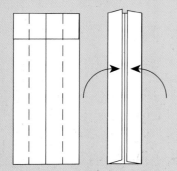

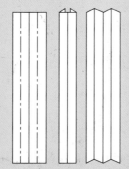

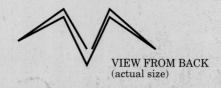

VIEW FROM BACK
(actual size)

STEP 3 Valley fold each side so that outer edges meet center crease, as shown.

STEP 4 Fold each side again using a mountain fold, so that outer edges meet center crease at back. Then adjust folds so that paper looks like an upside-down W, as shown.

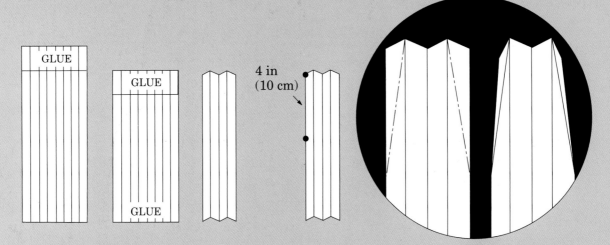

STEP 5 Unfold fuselage completely. Refold applying glue to contacting surfaces, as shown. Make sure fuselage is straight.

STEP 6 On each side, measure from top (front of fuselage), mark, and mountain fold along broken lines, as shown in enlarged view.

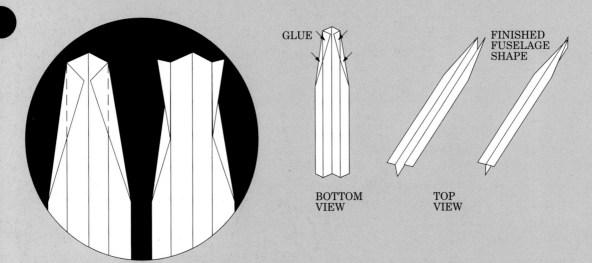

STEP 7 Flip over fuselage. On each side, valley fold triangle along broken lines, matching fold line to existing crease.

STEP 8 Glue triangles. Hold in place until glue sets. It is important that the fuselage stays straight. Do not glue nose yet.

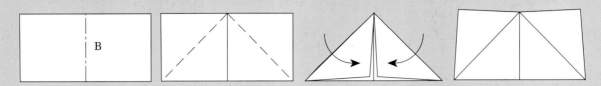

STEP 9   Use piece B to make the wings. Fold in half horizontally using a mountain fold. Unfold. On each side, valley fold diagonally so that upper edge meets center crease. Unfold.

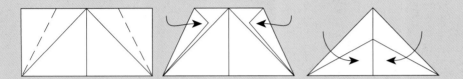

STEP 10   On each side, valley fold diagonally, so that outer edge meets previously made diagonal crease. Fold over again along the original diagonal creases.

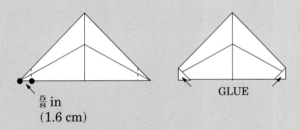

$\frac{5}{8}$ in
(1.6 cm)

GLUE

STEP 11   On each side, measure in from the wingtip and draw a line, indicated by broken line. Valley fold along this line. Glue the small triangle.

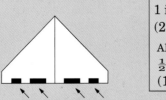

ELEVATORS
1 in x $\frac{1}{4}$ in
(2.5 cm x .6 cm)
AILERONS
$\frac{1}{2}$ in x $\frac{1}{4}$ in
(1.3 cm x .6 cm)

2 in
(5 cm)

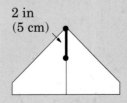

STEP 12   Flip wings over. On each side, in from the wingtip at the point of the triangles, make aileron on trailing (back) edge (see p 14). Make elevator adjacent to the aileron. Then cut a slit along center crease, as shown by heavy line.

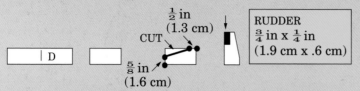

$\frac{1}{2}$ in (1.3 cm)

CUT

$\frac{5}{8}$ in (1.6 cm)

| D |

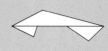

RUDDER
$\frac{3}{4}$ in x $\frac{1}{4}$ in
(1.9 cm x .6 cm)

STANDARD CANOPY
1 in x 3 in (2.5 cm x 7.5 cm)
with top point 2 in (5 cm)
from front tip

STEP 14 Use piece D to make the vertical tail. Valley fold in half vertically and glue together. Then measure and cut, as indicated by heavy line. Make rudder on trailing edge (see p 14).

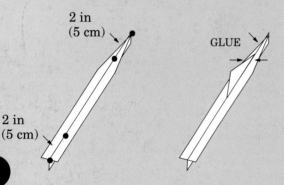

2 in (5 cm)

GLUE

2 in (5 cm)

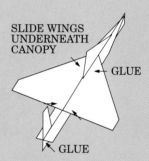

SLIDE WINGS
UNDERNEATH
CANOPY

GLUE

GLUE

STEP 15 Use piece C to make standard canopy (see p 30). Measure from front of fuselage, as shown, and make a mark for positioning the front of canopy. Measure from back of fuselage and make a mark for positioning the trailing edge of the wings. Apply glue to inside of nose and the small triangles on the bottom of canopy. Slide canopy in place and hold until glue sets.

STEP 16 Apply glue to wings and slide them underneath the canopy. Align trailing edge to the mark. Make sure wings are centered and at right angles to the fuselage. Then apply glue and slide vertical tail into back of fuselage so that trailing edges align.

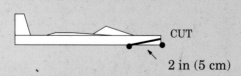

CUT

2 in (5 cm)

BACK VIEW

STEP 17 Measure and cut front of fuselage diagonally along heavy line to finish nose.

STEP 18 This airplane has no dihedral (upward slanting) or anhedral (downward slanting) of wings.

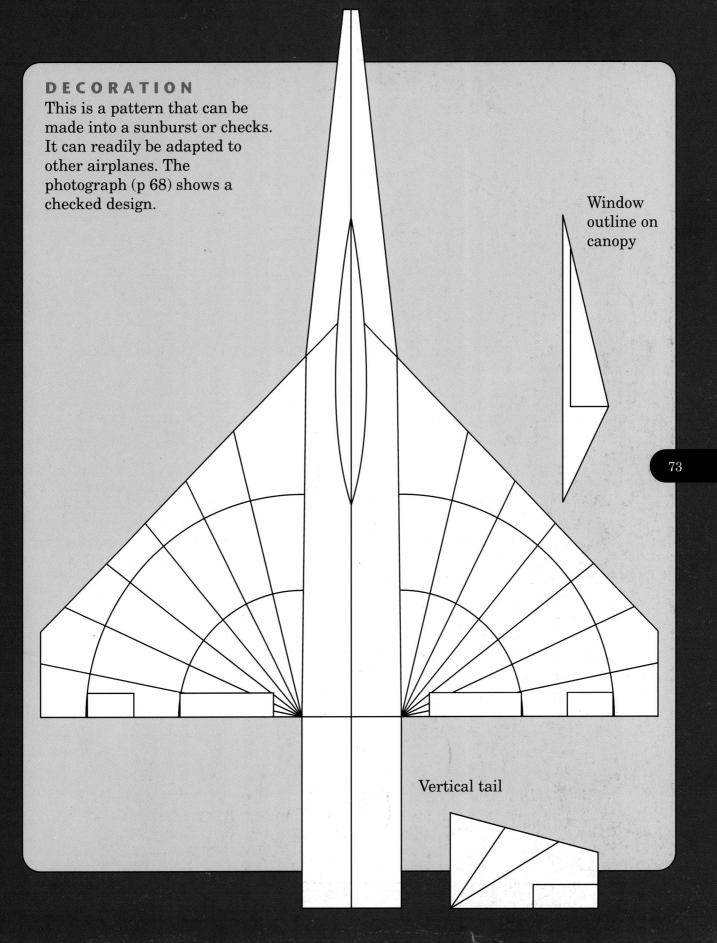

DECORATION

This is a pattern that can be made into a sunburst or checks. It can readily be adapted to other airplanes. The photograph (p 68) shows a checked design.

Window outline on canopy

Vertical tail

BACKGROUND INFORMATION

This paper airplane is called the "Tern" because its wings are turned forward, instead of being swept back, as is common. While the bird's wings are not swept forward, they are sharply bent. This paper airplane is modeled on the Grumman X29 experimental airplane, a plane that is controlled by on-board computers. In addition to having unusual wings, it is also a canard design.

MAKING THE AIRPLANE

This unusual airplane will fly fast and it is very maneuverable. Its construction is similar to the preceding four airplanes. This airplane is sensitive to pitch trim. Launch the plane by holding it between thumb and forefinger.

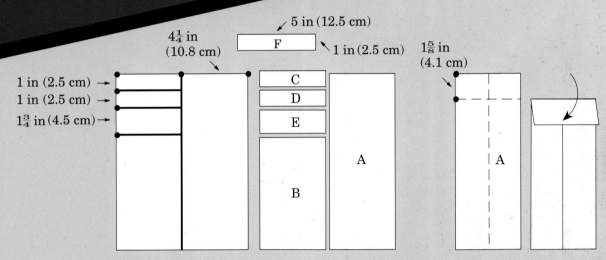

STEP 1 Measure and cut the various pieces from a sheet of bond paper. One additional piece is needed, as shown.

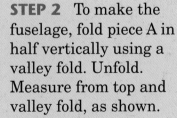

STEP 2 To make the fuselage, fold piece A in half vertically using a valley fold. Unfold. Measure from top and valley fold, as shown.

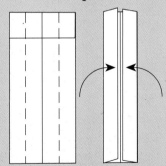

STEP 3 Valley fold each side so that outer edges meet center crease, as shown.

STEP 4 Fold each side again using a mountain fold, so that outer edges meet center crease at back. Then adjust folds so that paper looks like an upside-down W, as shown.

VIEW FROM BACK
(actual size)

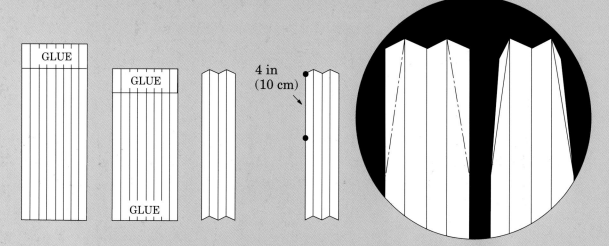

STEP 5 Unfold fuselage completely. Refold applying glue to contacting surfaces, as shown. Make sure fuselage is straight.

STEP 6 On each side, measure from top (front of fuselage), mark, and mountain fold along broken lines, as shown in enlarged view.

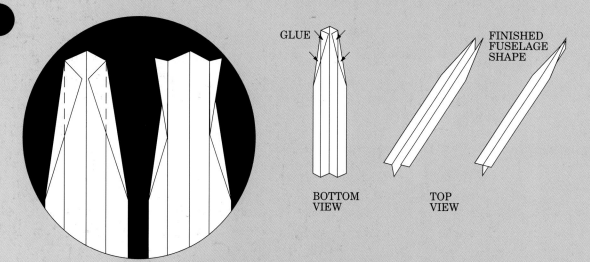

STEP 7 Flip over fuselage. On each side, valley fold triangle along broken lines, matching fold line to existing crease.

STEP 8 Glue triangles. Hold in place until glue sets. It is important that the fuselage stays straight. Do not glue nose yet.

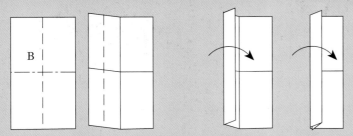

STEP 9 Use piece B to make the wings. Fold in half vertically, using a valley fold. Unfold. Fold in half horizontally using a mountain fold. Unfold. Then valley fold vertically so that one outer edge meets center crease. Fold over again along original vertical center crease.

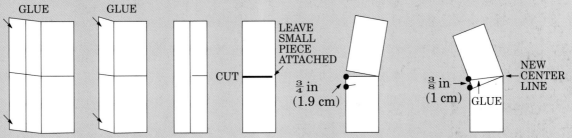

STEP 10 Unfold completely. Refold, applying glue to no more than 1 in (2.5 cm) from outer tips, as shown. The folded over part is the bottom of the leading edge (front) of the wings.

STEP 11 To sweep wings forward, cut along center line from the leading edge, leaving a small piece attached at the trailing (back) edge. Then measure and make a mark on leading edge, as shown. Align pieces to the mark. Glue. Measure and draw a new center line.

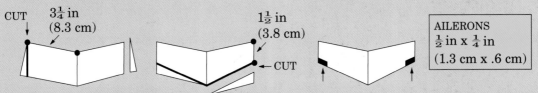

AILERONS
$\frac{1}{2}$ in x $\frac{1}{4}$ in
(1.3 cm x .6 cm)

STEP 12 To finish forward swept wings, measure and cut wing tips along heavy lines. Then cut trailing edge along heavy lines, as shown. On trailing edges, make ailerons (see p 14).

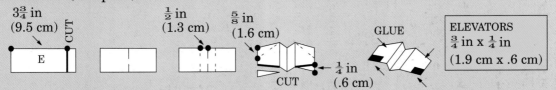

ELEVATORS
$\frac{3}{4}$ in x $\frac{1}{4}$ in
(1.9 cm x .6 cm)

STEP 13 Use piece E to make the canard wing. Cut to dimensions indicated. Valley fold in half vertically. Unfold. On each side, measure from center crease, as shown, and mountain fold. On each side, measure and mountain fold leading edge along broken lines. Glue. Cut trailing edges and make elevators (see p 14).

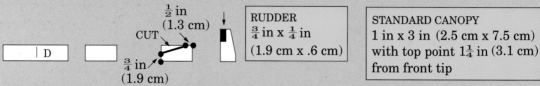

D

$\frac{1}{2}$ in
(1.3 cm)

CUT

$\frac{3}{4}$ in
(1.9 cm)

RUDDER
$\frac{3}{4}$ in x $\frac{1}{4}$ in
(1.9 cm x .6 cm)

STANDARD CANOPY
1 in x 3 in (2.5 cm x 7.5 cm)
with top point 1$\frac{1}{4}$ in (3.1 cm)
from front tip

STEP 14   Use piece D to make the vertical tail. Valley fold in half vertically and glue together. Then measure and cut along heavy line, as shown. Make rudder on trailing edge (see p 14).

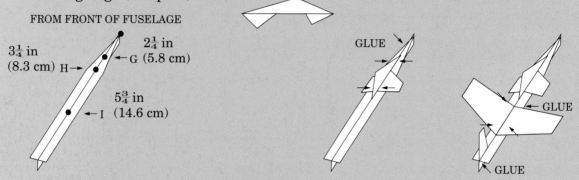

FROM FRONT OF FUSELAGE

3$\frac{1}{4}$ in
(8.3 cm) H →

2$\frac{1}{4}$ in
← G (5.8 cm)

5$\frac{3}{4}$ in
← I (14.6 cm)

GLUE

GLUE

GLUE

STEP 15   Use piece C to make standard canopy (see p 30). Measure from front of fuselage and make marks for positioning the leading edges of canopy at G, canard wings at H, and main wings at I, as shown.

STEP 16   Apply glue to inside of nose, the bottom of the canard wings, and the small triangles on the bottom of canopy. Slide in place together and hold until glue sets.

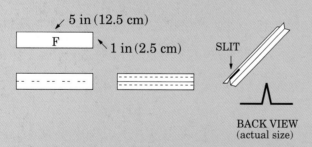

5 in (12.5 cm)

F

1 in (2.5 cm)

SLIT

BACK VIEW
(actual size)

STEP 17   Glue main wings in place, making sure they are centered and at right angles to the fuselage. Apply glue and slide vertical tail into back of fuselage so that trailing edges align.

STEP 18   Measure and cut a piece of paper F to dimensions shown. Mountain fold in half horizontally. Unfold. Then valley fold so that the outer edges meet center crease. Unfold. At one end, cut 1 in (2.5 cm) slit along center crease. Shape folds as shown.

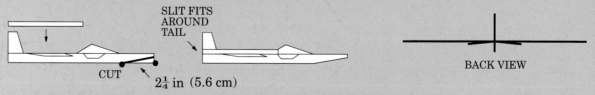

SLIT FITS
AROUND
TAIL

CUT

2$\frac{1}{4}$ in (5.6 cm)

BACK VIEW

STEP 19   Measure and cut nose diagonally along heavy line, as shown. Glue F onto top of fuselage, as shown, aligning at trailing edge.

STEP 20   Adjust wings to be level.

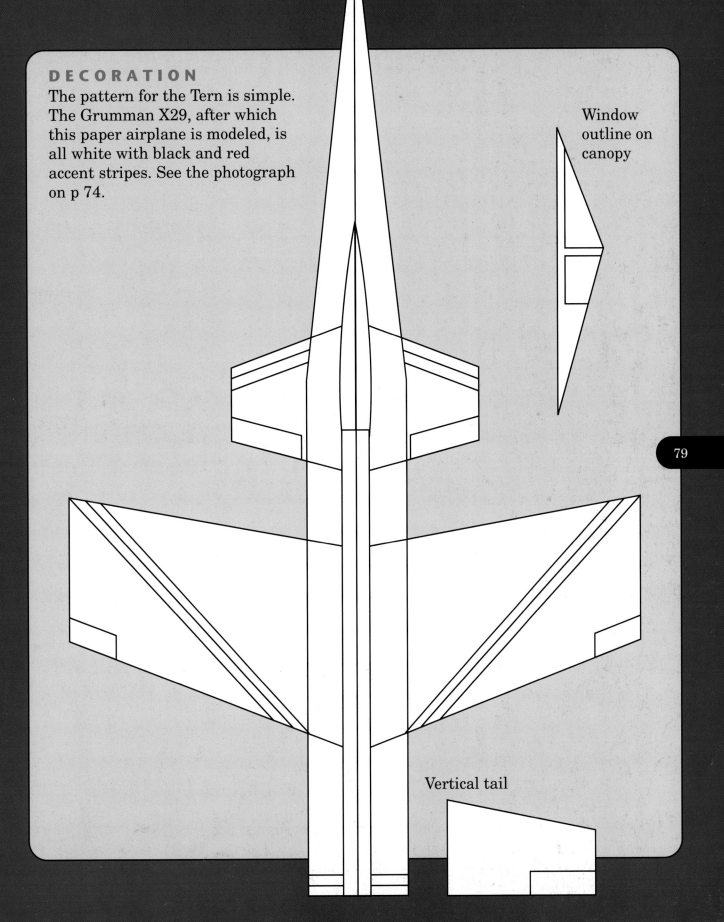

DECORATION

The pattern for the Tern is simple. The Grumman X29, after which this paper airplane is modeled, is all white with black and red accent stripes. See the photograph on p 74.

Window outline on canopy

Vertical tail

QUAIL

#16

BACKGROUND INFORMATION
This airplane is called the "Quail" because its short fuselage and short and blunt nose is similar to the bird. It has its wings quite far forward. The model does not fly fast or far, but it is aerobatic. It is modeled on aircraft having big radial engines, which accounts for the blunt nose. Such aircraft, like the Monocoupe 90 and the Stinson Reliant, were popular between the two world wars.

MAKING THE AIRPLANE

This is a conventional airplane design, having a fuselage, wings, and a tail with one vertical and two horizontal surfaces. Its very short nose makes it sensitive to pitch trim. It can be trimmed for level flight or aerobatic flight and can be flown indoors or out. Launch the plane by holding it between thumb and forefinger.

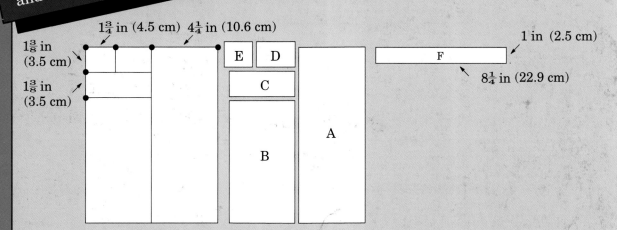

$1\frac{3}{4}$ in (4.5 cm) $4\frac{1}{4}$ in (10.6 cm)

$1\frac{3}{8}$ in (3.5 cm)

$1\frac{3}{8}$ in (3.5 cm)

1 in (2.5 cm)

$8\frac{1}{4}$ in (22.9 cm)

E D

C

A

B

F

STEP 1 Measure and cut the various pieces from a sheet of bond paper, as shown. One additional piece F is needed, as shown.

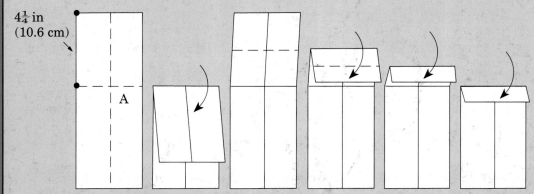

$4\frac{1}{4}$ in (10.6 cm)

A

STEP 2 To make the fuselage, fold piece A in half vertically using a valley fold. Unfold. Measure from top, as shown, and valley fold horizontally. Unfold. Then valley fold so that the upper edge meets horizontal crease. Again valley fold so that upper edge meets the crease. Then refold the original horizontal crease.

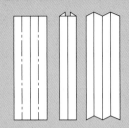

VIEW FROM BACK
(actual size)

STEP 3 Valley fold each side so that outer edges meet center crease, as shown.

STEP 4 Fold each side again using a mountain fold, so that outer edges meet center crease at back. Then adjust folds so that paper looks like an upside-down W, as shown.

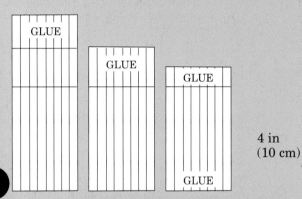

GLUE

GLUE

GLUE

GLUE

4 in
(10 cm)

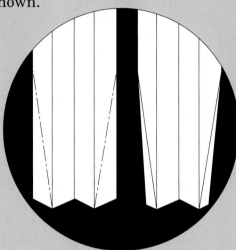

STEP 5 Unfold fuselage completely. Refold applying glue to contacting surfaces, as shown. Make sure fuselage is straight.

STEP 6 On each side, measure from bottom (back of fuselage), mark, and mountain fold along broken lines, as shown in the enlarged view.

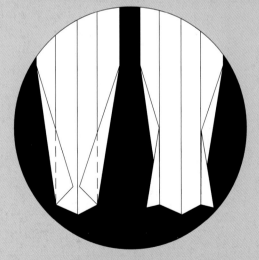

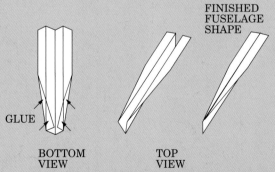

GLUE

BOTTOM
VIEW

TOP
VIEW

FINISHED
FUSELAGE
SHAPE

STEP 7 Flip over fuselage. On each side, valley fold triangle along broken lines, matching fold line to existing crease.

STEP 8 Glue triangles. Hold in place until glue sets. It is important that the fuselage stays straight. Do not glue nose yet.

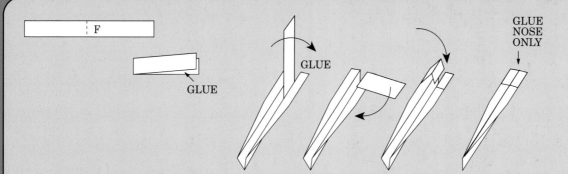

STEP 9 Use piece F to make the nose. Fold in half vertically, using a valley fold. Glue together. Applying glue to one side, insert F into nose and wrap entirely around the fuselage, as shown. Then glue fuselage together at nose only.

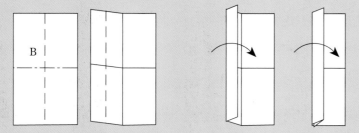

STEP 10 Use piece B to make the wings. Fold in half vertically, using a valley fold. Unfold. Fold in half horizontally using a mountain fold. Unfold. Then valley fold one side vertically so that one outer edge meets center crease. Fold over again along original vertical center crease.

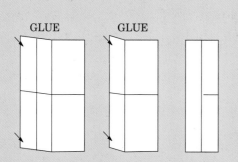

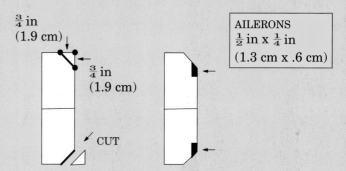

AILERONS
$\frac{1}{2}$ in x $\frac{1}{4}$ in
(1.3 cm x .6 cm)

STEP 11 Unfold completely. Refold, applying glue to no more than 1 in (2.5 cm) from outer tips, as shown. The folded over part is the bottom of the leading edge (front) of the wings.

STEP 12 To finish wings, measure and cut diagonals along heavy lines at the trailing (back) edges, as shown. Then make ailerons (see p 14).

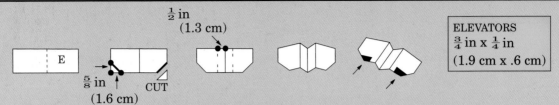

$\frac{1}{2}$ in (1.3 cm)

$\frac{5}{8}$ in (1.6 cm)

CUT

E

ELEVATORS
$\frac{3}{4}$ in x $\frac{1}{4}$ in
(1.9 cm x .6 cm)

STEP 13 Use piece E to make the horizontal tail. Valley fold in half vertically. Unfold. On each side, measure and cut diagonals on the trailing edge, as indicated by the heavy lines. On each side, measure from center crease, as shown, and mountain fold along broken lines. Make elevators on trailing edges (see p 14).

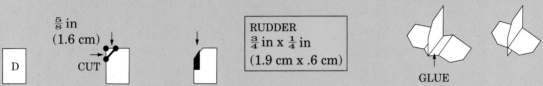

$\frac{5}{8}$ in (1.6 cm)

D

CUT

RUDDER
$\frac{3}{4}$ in x $\frac{1}{4}$ in
(1.9 cm x .6 cm)

GLUE

STEP 14 Use piece D to make the vertical tail. Measure and cut diagonal on trailing (back) edge, as shown. Make rudder on trailing edge (see p 14).

STEP 15 Join pieces D and E to finish tail. Apply glue and slide D into center of E, aligning trailing (back) edges.

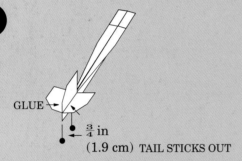

GLUE

$\frac{3}{4}$ in
(1.9 cm) TAIL STICKS OUT

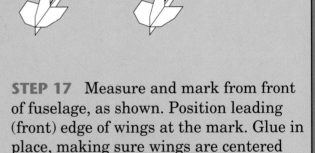

$1\frac{3}{8}$ in
(3.5 cm)

GLUE

STEP 16 Measure and mark along bottom of tail, as shown. Apply glue and slide tail into back of fuselage to the mark.

STEP 17 Measure and mark from front of fuselage, as shown. Position leading (front) edge of wings at the mark. Glue in place, making sure wings are centered and at right angles to the fuselage.

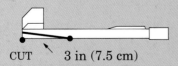

CUT   3 in (7.5 cm)

BACK VIEW

STEP 18 Measure and cut back of fuselage diagonally along heavy line to finish tail.

STEP 19 Adjust dihedral (upward slanting) of wings and horizontal tail, as shown.

84

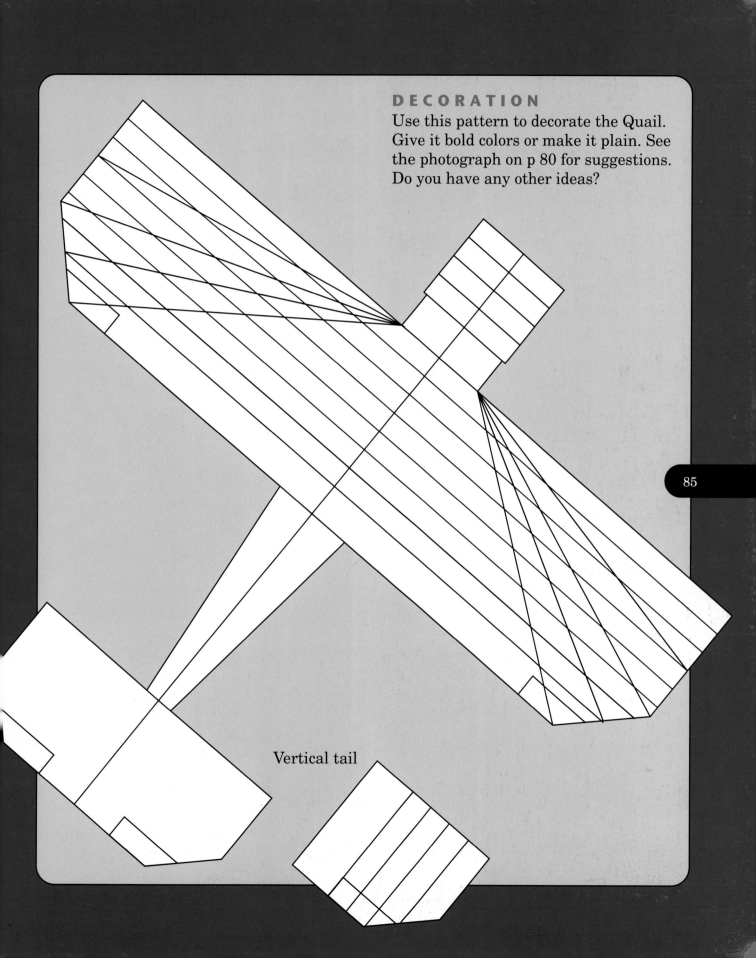

DECORATION

Use this pattern to decorate the Quail.
Give it bold colors or make it plain. See
the photograph on p 80 for suggestions.
Do you have any other ideas?

Vertical tail

HUMMINGBIRD

BACKGROUND INFORMATION

This airplane is called the "Hummingbird" because the rotary design of its wings is similar to the whir of the bird's rapidly beating wings. This paper helicopter is modeled after the small helicopters made by the Sikorsky, Bell, and Hughes companies. Because it has no engine this model cannot climb, but it can flutter downward, and is meant to be flown off a high balcony.

MAKING THE AIRPLANE

This design is of a single rotor helicopter. It cannot attain level flight, but will fly gently from a high balcony. Fly it indoors or out. Launch by holding it between thumb and forefinger, near the tail. First swing it around until the rotor begins turning, then let it go.

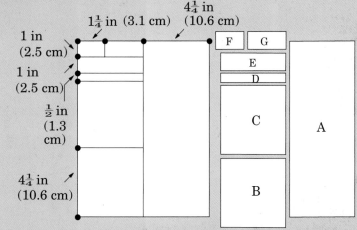

STEP 1 Measure and cut the various pieces from a sheet of bond paper, as shown. Discard C and G.

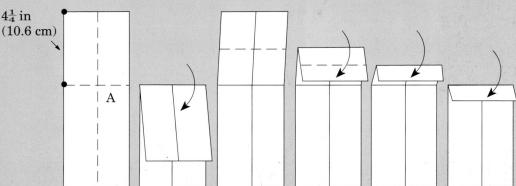

STEP 2 To make the fuselage, fold piece A in half vertically using a valley fold. Unfold. Measure from top, as shown, and valley fold horizontally. Unfold. Then valley fold so that the upper edge meets horizontal crease. Again valley fold so that upper edge meets the crease. Then refold the original horizontal crease.

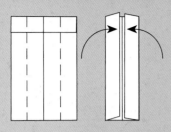 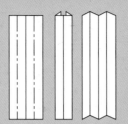 

VIEW FROM BACK
(actual size)

STEP 3 Valley fold each side so that outer edges meet center crease, as shown.

STEP 4 Fold each side again using a mountain fold, so that outer edges meet center crease at back. Then adjust folds so that paper looks like an upside-down W, as shown.

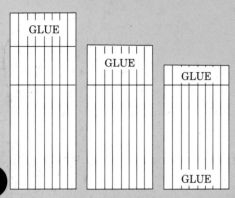

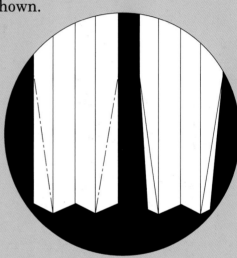

4 in (10 cm)

STEP 5 Unfold fuselage completely. Refold applying glue to contacting surfaces, as shown. Make sure fuselage is straight.

STEP 6 On each side, measure from bottom (back of fuselage), mark, and mountain fold along broken lines, as shown in the enlarged view.

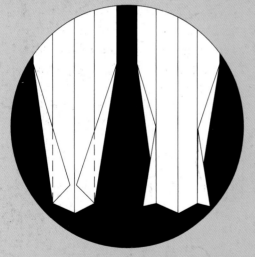

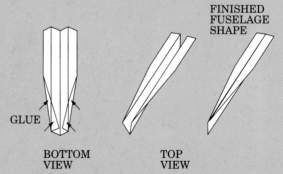

GLUE

FINISHED FUSELAGE SHAPE

BOTTOM VIEW

TOP VIEW

STEP 7 Flip over fuselage. On each side, valley fold triangle along broken lines, matching fold line to existing crease.

STEP 8 Glue triangles. Hold in place until glue sets. It is important that the fuselage stays straight. Do not glue nose yet.

88

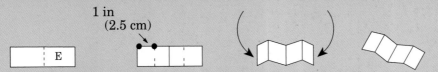

STEP 9 Use piece E to make the horizontal tail. Valley fold in half vertically. Unfold. On each side, measure from outer edge, as shown, and mountain fold. Adjust creases, as shown.

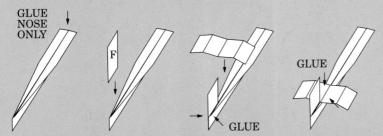

STEP 10 Glue the nose of the fuselage. Applying glue, slide the vertical tail F into the fuselage, aligning with the back of the fuselage. Then, applying glue to the horizontal tail, attach to fuselage just ahead of the vertical tail.

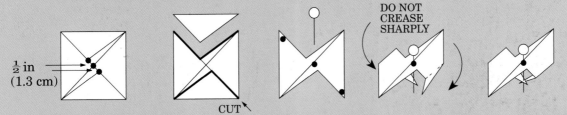

STEP 11 Use piece B to make the rotor. Using a ruler edge, draw diagonal lines across paper from opposite corners to find the center. On one of the diagonals, measure in both directions from the center, as shown. From these points, draw lines to the opposite corners, as shown. Cut out along heavy lines and discard pieces. Using a straight pin, make a hole at the center and in the two corner locations, as shown. Insert pin in center hole. Then mountain fold each corner, as shown, inserting pin through the second two holes. Do not crease sharply.

STEP 12 Use piece D to make the rotor driveshaft. Roll paper tightly, as shown, and glue. Place a pea-sized lump of plasticine on the top of the fuselage at the nose. Stick driveshaft into plasticine, with slight forward angle. Then insert pin through driveshaft into plasticine. Use plasticine for additional ballast, if needed.

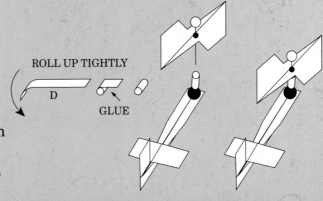

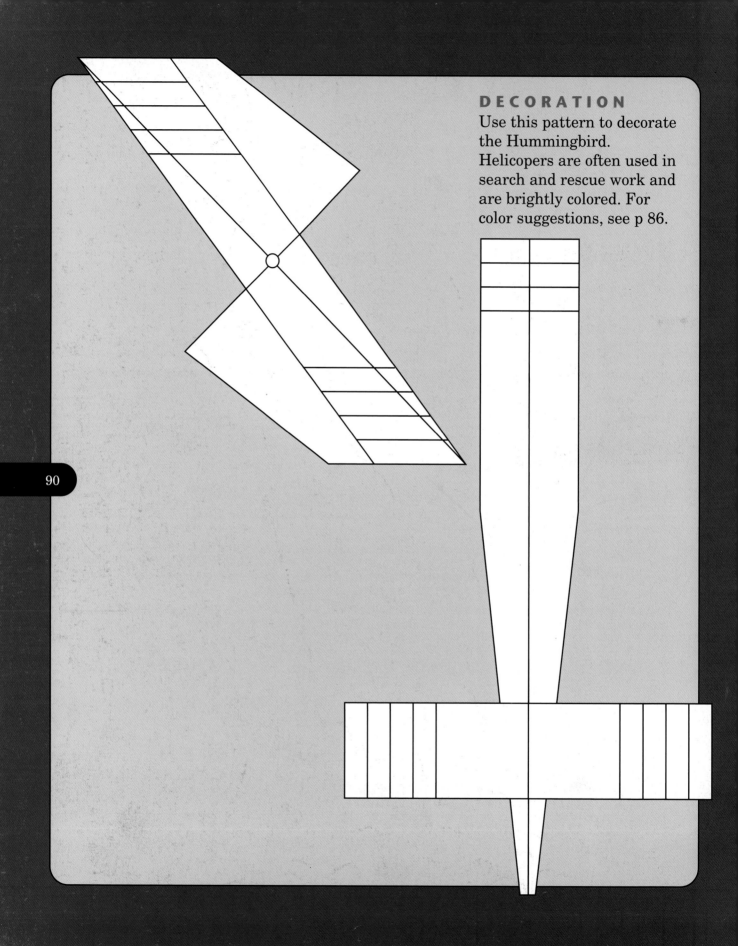

DECORATION
Use this pattern to decorate
the Hummingbird.
Helicopers are often used in
search and rescue work and
are brightly colored. For
color suggestions, see p 86.

NIGHTHAWK

#18

BACKGROUND INFORMATION

This airplane is called the "Nighthawk" because it is modeled on the Lockheed F117 Stealth, which is used primarily for nighttime military operations. It is not a fast airplane, but it is highly maneuverable. The unusual shape of the F117, together with its black color, are what make the airplane difficult to see, even by radar. This paper model has fine flying characteristics.

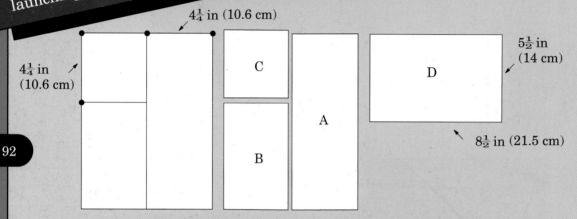

$4\frac{1}{4}$ in (10.6 cm)

$4\frac{1}{4}$ in (10.6 cm)

C

B

A

D

$5\frac{1}{2}$ in (14 cm)

$8\frac{1}{2}$ in (21.5 cm)

STEP 1 Measure and cut three pieces from a sheet of $8\frac{1}{2}$ in x 11 in (21.6 cm x 27.9 cm) paper. One additional piece is needed, as shown.

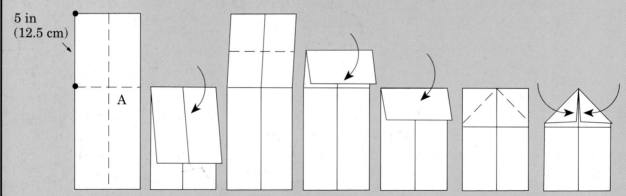

5 in (12.5 cm)

A

STEP 2 To make the fuselage, fold piece A in half vertically using a valley fold. Unfold. Measure from top, as shown, and valley fold horizontally. Unfold. Then valley fold so that the upper edge meets horizontal crease. Refold the original horizontal crease. Then on each side, valley fold diagonally so that top edge meets center crease.

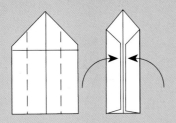
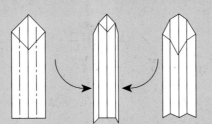

STEP 3 Valley fold each side so that outer edges meet center crease, as shown.

STEP 4 Fold again using a mountain fold, so that outer edges meet center crease at back. Then adjust folds so that paper looks like an upside-down W, as shown.

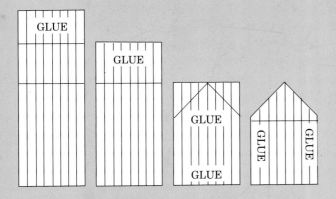

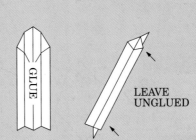

LEAVE UNGLUED

STEP 5 Unfold fuselage completely. Refold applying glue to contacting surfaces, as shown. Make sure fuselage is straight.

STEP 6 To finish fuselage, glue center of fuselage, leaving 2 in (5 cm) at the nose and 1 in (2.5 cm) at the tail end unglued.

½ in (1.3 cm)

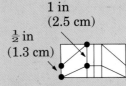
1 in (2.5 cm)
½ in (1.3 cm)

STEP 7 Use piece C to make the twin vertical tails. Fold in half horizontally using a valley fold. Glue sides together. Valley fold vertically. Unfold.

STEP 8 On each side, measure from center crease and mountain fold. Unfold, as shown. On each side, measure and draw lines, as shown.

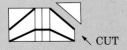
CUT

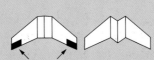

GLUE

RUDDERS
¾ in x ¼ in
(1.9 cm x .6 cm)

STEP 9 On each side, cut on heavy lines, as shown. Make rudders (see p 14). Adjust creases, as shown, and glue at center.

93

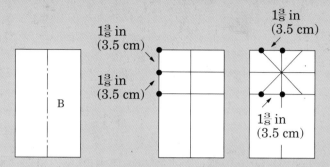

STEP 10 Use piece B to make the canopy. Fold in half vertically using a mountain fold. Unfold. On each side, measure and draw lines, as shown.

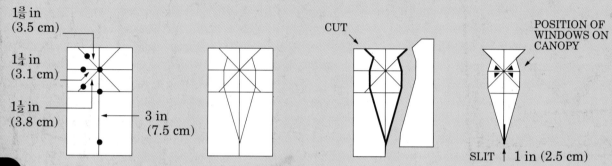

STEP 11 On each side, continue measuring and drawing lines. Then cut along heavy lines to make canopy outline, as shown. Make a slit at the bottom.

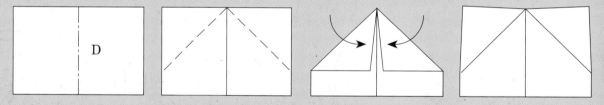

STEP 12 To finish canopy, mountain fold along diagonal and horizontal lines. Unfold. Fold again along original center crease, as shown. Then sink fold the front (see p 9). Glue front only.

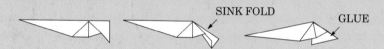

STEP 13 Use piece D to make the wings. Fold in half vertically using a mountain fold. Unfold. On each side, valley fold diagonally so that top edge meets center crease. Unfold.